THUS TO REVISIT

THUS TO REVISIT

SOME REMINISCENCES

BY

FORD MADOX FORD

" Parler des poètes est toujours une chose bien délicate, et surtout quand on la été un peu soi-même !"

1966

OCTAGON BOOKS, INC.

New York

Originally published 1921

Reprinted *1966*
by special arrangement with Janice Biala,
executrix of the Ford Madox Ford Estate

OCTAGON BOOKS, INC.
175 FIFTH AVENUE
NEW YORK, N. Y. 10010

Not for sale in the British Commonwealth of Nations

LIBRARY OF CONGRESS CATALOG CARD NUMBER: 66-17510

Printed in U.S.A. by
NOBLE OFFSET PRINTERS, INC.
NEW YORK 3, N. Y.

TO

MRS. G. D. H. COLE

WISHING SHE WOULD WRITE
MORE POEMS

CONTENTS

PART I

BEFORE MOONRISE

PART II

PROSATEURS

		PAGE
I.	Credentials	25
II.	*Puiser dans le Vide*	34
III.	The Lordly Treasure-House	41
IV.	*Mots Justes*	49
V.	*Combien je Regrette*	56
VI.	Coda	61
VII.	W. H. Hudson and the Simple Word	68
VIII.	Mr. Joseph Conrad and Anglo-Saxondom . . .	79
IX.	Henry James, Stephen Crane and the Main Stream .	102

PART III

THE BATTLE OF THE POETS

I.	"Thoughts before Battle".	129
II.	Mr. Pound, Mr. Flint, some Imagistes or Cubistes, and the Poetic Vernacular	143
III.	A Descriptive Interlude	169
IV.	"Vers Libre"	185
V.	Second Coda	216
	Index	225

PART I

BEFORE MOONRISE

"But when evening falls I go home and enter my writing room. On the threshold I put off my country habit, filthy with mud and mire and array myself in costly garments; thus worthily attired, and for four hours' space I feel no annoyance, forget all care; poverty cannot frighten me. . . . I am carried away."—N. Macchiavelli; *Letter to Francesco Vittori.*

I

WHAT follows is meant for the Uninstructed Reader.
The Uninstructed are not the Unintelligent. You
will find good natural—even peasant—intelligences
that, knowing nothing of the facts of a given case or
of a given branch of Knowledge, will yet, on the
facts being laid before them, arrive at surprisingly
just conclusions. On the other hand the Instructed
are only too often the unintelligent; when they are
not unintelligent they are only too often the wilfully
self-blinded. They make for safety, just as, a year
or so ago certain men made for safety by means of
the S.I.W.

It is a sad fact that too many—perhaps a majority
—of those who, having been instructed, instruct us
in turn, in Literature, do not know what those
letters mean. It is a fact sadder still that most of
those who know the significance of those majuscules
have little if any means of forming judgments as to
Literature. They love Books; they pass longish
hours in reading; but—as is to be awaited—the
temperaments of the above Instructed, render their
teachings disagreeable in manner and repulsive in
matter, to those accustomed to lives passed outside
studies lined with frequently unimportant and usually
not attractive, Printed Matter. We—the Writer
and such Readers as can be found to follow him on

3

a trip into dim regions—are setting out to discover how Literature stands, diminishes or holds her own in Anglo-Saxondom.

Printed Matter is another thing. Suppose you should see two poets fighting—as well you might see them fighting—in the King's Road, Chelsea; suppose you should mark their distorted visages, should be keenly alive to the atmosphere of that reputedly Bohemian, S.W.3 district of a great metropolis; should see the play of lamplight on the wind-swept golden hair and beard of the one, his sombrero, falling aside, making its last evolution on the wet asphalte of the roadway, like the wing of some brown, stricken sea-bird on a level, shining tide. Suppose you should mark the generous outline of the other, in the shadows, not the light, of the sordid, public illuminant; the eight dim reflections on his high hat, his silver headed cane raised in an attitude of self-defence, the high overtones of his claim for the protection of an absent police force. . . . Supposing that, at some subsequent date you should record vividly, even exaggeratedly, your impressions of the dim struggle—your rendering of the Affair would be Literature.

But if, on the other hand, some other fellow fifty years after the event should write in the *Literary Journal* of the 31/4/70:

"On the 31st of April, 1920, as has been hinted at in Literary Annals a lamentable assault was made by one P. upon Lawrence Queue. According to Professor Hauch eight blows were delivered on that occasion; according to Professor Bauch, eleven. Lawrence Queue as is well known to the world was an esteemed contributor to our columns. The identity of P. has long been wrapped in mystery, no more than his name having come down to Posterity along with a few negligible but popular verses. We are now able to cast some light on this sordid affair. The discovery by Professor Wauch of the University of Montana of the University Laundry Bills of that seat of Learning now enables us to state, the Professor having obligingly confided his discovery to us, that one P., was in 1893 an alumnus of that Alma Mater that has given to the world Professors. . . ."

That would be Printed Matter.

It is true that the Literary Journals of these Islands and of distant Continents will deny these premises. They will point to the fact that, in their pages and lists of received books, such things as collections of ana, of statistics and the chronicles of Societies of Embryology, are placed under the general heading of LITERATURE; therefore they must be Literature.

That sort of commercial exigency appears to be inevitable, But there is no established Literary-Technical language in Anglo-Saxondom and no Chartered Body established to settle what words are or are not distinguished by certain significances. Let us then, Writer and Reader together agree as follows:

A vivid account by an eyewitness of the campaigns of the first Duke of Marlborough; an inspiring Ode on those campaigns in whatever metre; a lyric such as that beginning:

"Oh, Polly love, oh Polly love, the Route has just begun
And I must march away to the beating of the drum,"

or a re-construction in words of the scenery round Ypres with one of John Churchill's scarlet and white columns trailing across it—all these things would be Literature. But a statistical account of the ordnance in Malbrouk's Army or a tabulation of the vowels in "OH POLLY LOVE!" would not be Literature, though written by a Professor of Poetry and printed at an University Press. Such things it is convenient to call Printed Matter. Or, indeed, let us not bother our heads about such things. Let our moony province be solely what used to be called the Litterae Humaniores, and let us leave all dealings with, and even the naming of all other appearances in Print to be used, according to their special purposes, by the Critics of the Periodical Press, the Universities and the High Schools.

I imagine my friend the Uninstructed Reader asking:

"But why bother our heads about Literature, if this indeed and not the other, be Literature? *This* Literature is, isn't it? the product of an Art. We are taught at school and in all our contacts with Life since our schooldays we have learned to regard the Arts with deep suspicion. With all the deference in the world let us say that, if we practised an Art instead of studying for a Profession we should make no money. So our fathers have told us. . . . And indeed our fathers have told us, too, that, if we have any truck with artists we shall become bad men of Business; the profits from our old-established Bucket-Shop which dates from the reign of the Third William, will fall off; we shall become physically flabby; we shall commit acts of immorality and end in the Divorce or the Police Courts."

That is not necessarily the case. And even if it were, let the Reader consider, before throwing down this book! The Arts are very old things, performing in Society very ancient functions—and these days, like all other days since last rose-crowned kings played upon flutes of gold, are extraordinarily fraught

with the perils, overshadowed by the loom, of Violent
Change. The Reader's Business may well fail to show
all its old profit of 111 per cent. per annum if he allow
contact with the Arts to numb his avidity. (That is
certainly what contact with the Arts will do for
him!) On the other hand if Something or Other do
not diminish avidity in him and his fellows, it will be
a very short time indeed before the Reader finds
himself as naked as any bourgeoise of the Government of Kieff.

And that something or other can only be the
knowledge of what song the Syrens sang; or, if you
prefer it, of the Sermon on the Mount. . . . For such
things alone can give you knowledge of the hearts,
the necessities, the hopes and the fears of your fellow
men; and such knowledge alone can guide us through
life without disaster.

To put the matter at its simplest:

It is pretty certain—indeed we may say it is
absolutely certain!—that Prussia would not have
made war upon a large portion of the world had
Prussia understood the nature of the men of those
regions. Take Anglo-Saxondom alone: Prussia
would have better understood the nature of Anglo-
Saxondom had our Anglo-Saxon Literature been
better—had it indeed been so good that every
Prussian must have read a great number of Anglo-
Saxon books instead of merely the works of the late
Oscar Wilde! But Statistics and Printed Matter
had convinced Prussia that, at any rate the Eastern
branch of the unvoiced race, had a falling trade, a
diminishing birthrate, a negligible Army, a Navy
that might *just* be chanced. . . . But, in these things,
national psychologies are the dominant factors and,

as foundations for the study of psychologies, statistics are of little service. For that, Creative Literature alone can serve.

But our Creative Literature, as distinct from that of all the rest of the world, is usually the work of happy-go-lucky and doctrinairely obstinate Amateurs all whose practice is the recording of their own moods of exaltation rather than the rendering of exact observation of Life or even of Manners. So our Creative Literature is neglected by other races used to a stronger meat and shunned by our own people who have gradually come to regard all Literature as something anæmic when it is not repellent. . . .

That is a side of the matter that the Reader will find abundantly worked out in later chapters. For the moment let us examine the frame of mind of what we will call the Enemy Forces. This frame of mind is put in an excellent nutshell in a letter addressed by an Eminent Novelist to the *English Review*, in which periodical this book appeared in serial form. The material portion of this letter will be found in a footnote to a subsequent page. It is enough here to state that this Eminent Novelist in this letter advocates writing by inspiration alone ; decries all those who analyse literary methods, damns the late Henry James ; calls—in what would appear to be the current fashion of conducting literary controversies—the Present Writer a liar and a parasite —and deprecates all appraisement of Literary greatnesses. . . .

Yet, six months, or less, after this letter was written the hoardings of London displayed immense posters styling this Eminent Novelist : EARTH's GREATEST WRITER ! That, of course, was not the fault of Earth's Greatest Writer. But it only shows

how difficult it is for most of us—even for those most
chary of appraisement—to avoid being appraised by
some one or other. It might or might not be better
if all books were published, like Army Council Instructions, merely with reference numbers: L.C.I.,
2/4/21, Nov. 17543 " Thus to &c." But books are
not so published and it would seem to be better for
the world if such appraisements of Literary Greatness
as are performed should be the work of others than
the advertising managers of Sunday newspapers.

Be that as it may, this Letter puts very felicitously
the view of their profession held by what it is convenient to call the Typical English Writer of the pre-
Moonrise period. You sit down; you write; the
vine leaves are in your hair; you forget mundane
tribulations; gradually intoxication steals over you.
Sometimes you stumble into sense; sometimes you
do not. You may end as Earth's Greatest Writer on
the posters—but your work will contain, almost
certainly, great passages of an amateurish dullness.
That is probably why, for the world outside Anglo-
Saxondom, English Literature is represented by Lord
Byron and the late Oscar Wilde.

II

The rising of the moon came, exactly a hundred
years ago, when there appeared in this planet Gustave
Flaubert and his circle. These were the first writers
to make and to formulate the discovery that the first
study of the writer must be the Reader.

And let not the present Reader of these present
pages be dragged from that consideration by the

Protean attacks of any misrepresenters. Post-Flaubertian " technique " is just the purest common-sense. It has nothing to do with Revolution, with license or even with Freedom. It is Discipline. It enjoins a strict study of language so that the writer may not be a bore ; it enjoins a strict study—an appraisement !—of past works that have interested humanity so that the Writer may be as interesting as possible to as many readers as possible. Of course the Writer—every Writer—cannot interest every Reader. But he can make the effort not to bore readers of potential goodwill.

That is again matter to be later elaborated. . . . For at this point the Reader is crying out :

" What is all this ? " He will continue, by asking whether all artists do not seek to please Readers or purchasers so as to gain great sums of money. But that is far from being the case. Some Artists care nothing for money ; some care very little. Some—and perhaps these, in Anglo-Saxondom are far the greater number—care a great deal for money but care nothing at all for the Reader. You may say that they have for the Reader—whom they call " the Public "—a morbid hatred ; and their settled, gloomy conviction is that the Reader, the Public, should be coerced, municipally or otherwise, into the perusal of their works. . . . So, from within themselves they spin conventions that they clothe with obscure language. . . . And these half-Artists are the real pests of Literature ; they are the purveyors of the eternally second-rate ; after their suicides, on their poor mouldering remains pullulate the dreaded Intelligentsia. It is because Anglo-Saxondom has produced always too many of these that Literature in the

Western world performs no noticeable function, has
no place in the hearts of its nations and is a thing
now purely provincial to the lands of its origins.

These then, are the second rate. . . . They give
birth to that vast breed who, having no gifts save
industry and the determination to wear black coats
and linen collars, achieve doctorates, knighthoods, and
professional chairs—following a Profession more
pompous, but not more dignified or more useful than
that of the Stamp Collector. This is the process:

A poet chooses to call Primrose Hill the NEW
JERUSALEM; to call policemen THOTH; worthy
citizens, THEL; burglars HETH; usurers, THURIM—
and so on through an epic immensity. Apart from
these imbecilities our Poet is truly somewhat of a
poet. He starves; tears up half his manuscripts;
attempts suicide; is taken to an asylum. He dies.
Twenty years later along comes the typical Critic of
English · Literature. (But, in between, some good
fellow of an artist will have seen beauties under the
obscurities and with the Artist's generosity will have
trumpeted these for twice what they were worth.
Perhaps, he will even have soothed the dying hours
of our poor second rate poet.) The typical English
Critic will make a map of Primrose Hill; will write
theses on the word-roots of Thoth, Thel, Heth and
Thurim; will write a volume on the washing bills of
the poet's mother, re-discovered in Reading; will
measure and record with exactitude the dimensions
and appointments of the cell in which dies our poet;
will print, analyse, parse and annotate the love-
letters of the poet's illiterate *fiancée*. So he will
come to his Academic fauteuil!

For there will be an infinite company of such

Typical English Critics and these, being good fellows all, up to a point, will hob and nob, snuffle, toast each other, elect each other by order of least resistance and seniority to this or that post of honour or of profit. . . . That is Academicism—the thing that five generations of the Writer's ancestry have ruined themselves in attempting to destroy !

The Reader will say :

" But these pursuits appear to be innocent. You say that these coteries are self-helping Brotherhoods akin to the Guilds by which, we are told, Society is to be saved. . . . Besides, what is all this to me ? "

Alas. . . .

Literature is a pleasant thing, an alluring thing ; a thing of amusement—and of Salvation. There are innumerable beautiful books of which the Reader will never have heard—because of the towering, forbidding Mountain of Printed Matter, the mole-work of this Coffee and Commercial Room of the Inn of Letters. The Reader will have had his enjoyment of a few very beautiful books killed for ever because, when he was at school an " English " Master, aiming at ultimate admission to that Coffee-Room Club, will have seized him, the poor little, blubbering Readerlet, by the back of the neck and will have crammed his mouth with dust, settled in Libraries, on volumes of Shakespeare. So the Reader will have grown up, hating the Humaner Letters, semi-barbarous, at home incult and, in the mass of him, derided abroad. . . .

And that is a lamentable thing—for the English Reader is a kind, good, inarticulate and gently poetic being. Only he has so few to " voice " him. . . . And the Typical English Writer claims the right—or

advances that it is his sole duty—to write what he
" wants " in a ceaseless flow of self-intoxication.

Now a man writing "what he wants" is always
in great danger. Sometimes he may amuse, titillate,
even awaken thought. Sometimes he will do none
of these things. Then he will bore—but bore to
distraction ! And the shadow of that boredom will
lie over huge passages, whole tracts of his pages, to
right and to left. So, according as the writer's
dominant proportion of passages is attractive or un-
attractive, he will take his place in the ranks of
the Immortals. This is true of all pre-Flaubertian
Writers. . . .

At this point the Reader will hear an immense
noise. That will be innumerable dead Academicians
turning in their graves ; that will be innumerable
Reviewers shaking their Fountain Pens so that rivers
of denigrating ink may flow over the head of this
poor Writer ; that will be a simultaneous uprising of
a whole Forty Thousand Immortals who shall exclaim
in unison :

"What ! This fellow denies Greatness to Homer,
Virgil, Petrarch, Shakespeare, Pope, Fielding, Milton,
Wordsworth, Dickens, Scott, Tennyson, Lamb,
Hazlitt, Robert Louis. . . ."

This fellow denies greatness to no one. He is
merely trying to point out that, in the works of
all pre-Flaubertian Anglo-Saxon writers there are
passages of dullness ; and that the aim of writers
to day must of necessity be the elimination of such
passages from their works. That is all it amounts to.

The matter is easy to put convincingly. Let the
Reader have a very vocal friend. In listening to him
the Reader will be pleased by certain passages of

talk ; bored—possibly even extremely irritated—by certain other passages in which tautologies, inexact phrases, repetitions or a too great indulgence in personal idiosyncrasies, are indulged in by that friend. Supposing then that the Reader have certain gifts or suffrages to bestow—votes for an Almshouse or so on.   His friend will be a wise man, if, eschewing for the time his passionate delight in the ravishing sound of his own voice, he study the Reader to see what manner of talk will please him—if he eliminate his tautologies and repetitions, if he try after exactitude of phrase and abandon for the moment his more irritating personal mannerisms.   For, if he bore and bore and bore through many long interviews, though he have never so much of an unused faculty to please, never so much of a good case or never so improving a personality, it is ten chances to one that the Reader will bestow his favours elsewhere.   Wordsworth was an exquisite poet of six hundred lines.   But he wrote what Tom Sawyer called mornamillion, so that for one reader who searches him through to-day, five hundred thousand are " choked off "—their gorges literally rising at the thought of the eternity of dusty lines that Wordsworth wrote in the self-intoxication of his scratching pen.   That is a great pity—but it is the whole story in a nutshell !

Literary Ability in fact, is not the same thing as the Literary Sense ; since the Literary Sense implies the power of self-criticism as well as the power to learn from others.   The one has always existed : the other is a comparatively new-born thing, arising from a new and growing necessity.   For, as the world, with its new powers of multiplication of books, has become more and more full of Print, the despised

Public has grown more and more impatient of *longueurs,* more and more avid of good workmanship. A public may never have read the stories of Maupassant—but the mere existence of Maupassant in the world makes impossible the reading of ARTAXERXES or GUZMAN D'ALFARACHE. Post-Flaubertian technique amounts to no more than a determination on the part of the artist not to nod as, some Academicist has told us, Homer sometimes did. The Writer of to-day must be self-critical or he will not be read even though he possess a most beautiful talent. It is no use for the Academic critic to say : " Look at our esteemed fellow-contributor Lawrence Queue. He writes by inspiration. *He* is famous ; he contributes a weekly column to the *Literary Journal!* " Mr. Queue's poems sell two thousand copies ; his name is known to fourteen thousand people : the literate population of the British Isles alone numbers over forty million souls. If then Mr. Queue is a great poet the inhabitants of these Islands are barbarous. The Writer hesitates to lay this charge against his fellow countrymen : it seems at least more patriotic to say that the boot is on the other leg.

And, for sure, the boot is on the other leg ! Its last pulling on, as the Writer has witnessed it, as the subject matter of this book of Reminiscences. It describes, principally, how beautiful talents are reported for dead, or in the alternative, led captive at the wheels of Vested Academicists—and beautiful talents are the desperate need of these sad months and years when we tremble on the verge of a return to barbarism. . . .

In order to establish his right to talk, really

diffidently enough, on these matters, the Writer may
as well advance the claim that the greater part of his
conscious life has been spent in the effort to help the
cause of one beautiful talent or another—seeking on
the whole to limit his championings to such talents
as seemed likely to flow between the main-streams of
European Literature. For there is such a mainstream which, ignoring frontiers and boundaries,
flows, for all the world like a river on the map, in a
serpentine course, over mountain systems, marine
channels, and across Oceans—through Time. Let us
say that it began with Cervantes and Lope da Vega
—or, if you like, earlier still with the Troubadours
and Troveres who influenced the verse-forms of
Chaucer. Or, if you like, put its source later, with
those Italians from whom the Elizabethans translated
or plagiarised. . . . Let us, however, limit our survey
to the latest of all the Arts—that of the Novel. . . .
For that we must begin with Cervantes and Lope da
Vega. This Art died in Spain ; but the Picaresque
novel lived again in England in the novels of Defoe.
The influence of Defoe passed to France—if you
like to put it so, it passed to France through the
channels of the, semi-bourgeois, romantic narratives
in the *Spectator*, and these begot the *Marianne*
of Marivaux. *Marianne* may or may not have be-
gotten *Pamela :* it is an open question whether
Richardson's first novel was or was not an imitation
of Marivaux's. . . . At any rate Richardson's subsequent influence on France was overwhelming.
Rousseau wrote his essay in the manner of *Clarissa ;*
Diderot's *Le Neveu de Rameau* was intended to
be taken as claiming that Richardson was on a
better road than that of Euripides ; and in the

'forties of last century French criticism, official or of the school of Musset, proclaimed *Clarissa* to be the finest novel in the world. The spiritual children, then, of Richardson were Diderot and the French Encyclopædists who loved middle-class Realism ; these begot Chateaubriand and Stendhal who paid attention to exactitude of language. The stream passed to Flaubert, Maupassant, Turgenev—the first really conscious writers. So the Literary Sense was born. . . .

That its disturbance passed quickly to these shores there was evidence enough in the 'nineties ; across the Atlantic there was evidence enough still earlier. At that point this Writer will be found to begin his more minute inspection. But the Reader has only to go through the desperately High Falutin' critical writings of Stevenson to see the leaven at work. And indeed Stevenson was a writer conscious enough : even his most Academic supporter will not deny it! Temperamentally he may, as Stephen Crane said, have done enormous harm to the English novel—but he killed for good the dreadfully unformed and uninvented stuff that our grandfathers had to be content with, and the poor old public will no longer even sniff at a story of adventure that is *much* worse in construction than, let us say, *Kidnapped*. That was probably the work of Henley. For, since Stevenson wrote languid words of official condemnation for the " French Realists," the children of Defoe and Richardson, he can certainly not be accused of ignoring the other side of the Channel. Henley was much more aware, as a critic, of the queer Spanish-English-French-English-Russian-French origins, the International criss-crossing, that have gone to the

makings of modern art. It was he—he first called
Henry James " Henrietta Maria "—who first printed
Mr. Conrad's work in serial form. And with Mr.
Conrad and Henry James the Mainstream again
washed the shores of the Atlantic. This impinge-
ment which synchronised with the Writer's conscious
literary life he is about to describe.

III

The writer does not apologise for the fact that
this book takes the form of REMINISCENCES rather
than that of HISTORY. To arrogate to oneself the
title of Historian is to lay claim to Impartiality—
and this is a book of Propaganda.

Certain events took the Writer—as whom didn't
they take?—into fields far different from those of the
Intrigue in which most of his life had been passed.
Coming back to a world more normal he employed
himself in other avocations. . . . Then, as the
Reader will see, came a serious call once more to
revisit the glimpses of the moon. . . . The breed-
ing of what Large Black Pig or the evolving of what
Disease Proof Potato could resist it?

It is true that the Call was to do no more than
make a survey of where British Imaginative Literature stands to-day. But one is human. It is all very
well to ape Cinna and, planting one's cabbages, to
ignore all public omens. But once one is tempted
from green tranquillities, it is not easy to close one's
ears to the groans of the Body-Politic. And who
will deny that to-day the Republic groans in all its
members? Indeed, despair can seldom have been so

general in a State not immediately menaced by Fire, Famine, Pestilence or Strife in Arms !

So there re-awakened in the Writer the passionate belief that Creative Literature—Poetry—is the sole panacea for the ills of harassed humanity—the sole alleviator, the only healing unguent. For Creative Literature is the only thing that can explain to man the nature of his fellow men ; and a great, really popular Art, founded on, and expressive of a whole people, is the sole witness of the non-barbarity of a Race. But to do, and to be this, an Art must be an exact, not an intoxicated, occupation and Artists must be self-less. In Writers that exactness of vision and that self-lessness have been things of slow growth—but they have grown, however, slowly. The Writer bears witness to this growth for a quarter-century or so.

It is witness neither encyclopædic nor all-embracing, Those who wish for an insular glorification of the British School will say that this is indeed the play of Hamlet without the Prince of Denmark. . . Let it then be the History of Fortinbras : the work of one who waited for the coming of the Dublin Abbey Theatre in the days of Sir Henry Irving at the old Lyceum ! So that these are a craftsman's notes, the fruits of an observation merely personal. For you cannot "document" the figures or the tendencies of your own day. Only hearsay evidence is at your disposal—and hearsay is a dangerous thing on which to rely. . . .

There remain two minor points :

For the bulk of the book the Writer has employed the First Person—just here and there employing this indirect form to show that he can do it. The " I "

form has the advantage of letting you do without
periphrases.   But one loses a certain impressive
Pomposity, gaining however in irritant power and
being a boon to the Reader.   The " I " form is
nevertheless much the more difficult : you have to be
for ever on the watch to prevent the creeping in of
aspects of immodesty.   To say : " The Writer may
claim that it is in part owing to his exertions that a
certain Noxious Fowl no longer haunts the purlieus
of Academe," is be-wigged and very awful.   You
may print that.   To write : " I killed Cock Robin "
simply cannot be done.   So the personal narrative
calls for unceasing gymnastics—and sometimes, since
it is weary work suffering fools for ever gladly -- one
omits such saltations !

Again :

Here is a constant source of speculation to the
Writer : Why is it that you may say worse than
hang—much worse than hang in print of any poor
dead man whereas it is considered the worst of taste
to write, in Reminiscences, of the Living?   Of
any one in a Cemetery you may say that his mother
was a prostitute and his own life passed in bilking
landladies—and the *Literary Journal* will applaud
your industry.   But if you accuse Mr. X of splitting
an infinitive across the dinner-table, you become a
pariah for that Organ.   That is mysterious, for it is
surely more courageous to give a man a chance to
reply to you.   It is certainly more brave.   If the
writer accuse Mr. Y of plagiarising from Martin
Tupper the world is surely benefited by the fact that
Mr. Y is able to reply—and to prove, if he can—that
he has never read a word of that philosopher.

Mysterious !   Or perhaps it isn't.   Perhaps it is

merely the Herd-Sense—the dislike felt by the Herd
for individual acts of bravery. One puts on protective armour oneself—every kind of protective
armour ; so one dislikes the spectacle of one warrior
going naked into battle and slaying his thousands.
Pope, we are told, was ostracised for writing the
Dunciad.

Of course there is the muddled conviction—which
the Writer instinctively shares—that the living can
feel pain whereas the Dead cannot. That is an anti-
social instinct, none the less. It may be painful for
Mr. X to be reminded that he splits his infinitives :
but if he is not hauled up he will go on doing it and
so corrupt our little children that round the table
go. . . .

Still, the Writer is only human and hates to give
pain to any save Academicists—and even to them he
would give, to each, a great big pension, reams of
paper, a whole library, a printing press—and an
incinerator. Thus this book has its lacunæ, its
gentlemen indicated by letters of the alphabet. For
the Eminent are, if they aren't anything else,
eminently touchy. They are used to be addressed
as, to consider themselves, demi-gods : you must not
poke fun at them or, either they will cry, or, as in the
case of the Eminent Letter Writer at whom we have
glanced, they will seek to kick you in the stomach.
That is a pity.

The fault lies really with the Periodical Press.
The writers of reviews have so few adjectives. You
may put it that they cry " God-like ! God-like !
God-like ! " all the day so that the least meritorious of
the merely distinguished get exactly the same praise
as and come to feel themselves on a level with, Dante,

Homer, Aeschylus, and Milton—Earth's Greatest Writers.

So the Writer begs the Reader to keep in mind this one thing : It is not want of generosity but a desire to keep some sense of proportion that prevents the Writer from saying every time that he mentions a living brother of the pen: This is EARTH'S GREATEST WRITER ! For this writer remembers almost always Catullus, Petrnious, Shakespeare, Flaubert, and Turgenev.

As for the rights and wrongs of reporting conversations whether of the living or the dead, the following is the code of ethics of the Writer : If a public man—and Authors are public men—talk whether in Public or in Private of the principles of his public work, he must expect to be reported, and it is his duty to talk with reasonable care and sincerity of that public subject. A priest would expect to be reported and dealt with if he talked bawdy or heretically to his parishioners or fellow soggarts in the streets: the functions of an author are no less sacerdotal when he is discussing his Art. To report details of private history, affections or intimacies is usually infamous—unless, like Boswell, you should be paying public tribute to a figure whom you have much loved.

PART II

PROSATEURS

"'There is only one art of writing and that is the art of poetry ; and, whenever you feel the warmth of human experience in any writing, there is poetry, whether it is in the form we call prose, or in rhyme and metre, or in the unrhymed cadence in which the greater part of this book is written. . . ."—F. S. FLINT, Preface to *Otherworld*.

1

CREDENTIALS

LAST year, the conductors of a serious American journal, very flatteringly, asked me to contribute to their columns a *compte rendu* of the English literary world at the present moment. I seized at the opportunity—at first gladly and certainly with gratitude. For, about January, 1914, the Vorticists, Cubists, Imagistes, and Futurists having told me that *I* was Impressionism and that Impressionism was dead, I took my formal farewell of Letters, quite sincerely, in some magazine or other—I think it was *The Thrush*. Then came the war, and I wrote a great deal of Propaganda in French and English. So it was with pleasure that I contemplated, an insubstantial ghost, revisiting the light of a moon I had purposed never to see again.

That particular moon shines over our own Parnassus—the ungrassed slopes on the northern bank of the Thames. The reader may not know them : they stretch over monticules and concealed valleys. Let him, then, mount Bedford Street from the Strand. Exploring the neighbourhood of Covent Garden Market, ten to one he will see several of our Immortals issuing from doorways and buttoning fat cheques into comfortable breast-pockets. There is also Paternoster Row. Alas ! in those *parages* the

streets are narrow and the houses relatively high. So
that, on moonlight nights there, he will catch only
glimpses of our chaste Dian. . . .

And the conductors of that Magazine asked me,
formally, to treat of (Messrs.)

" Gosse	Yeats	Sinclair (Miss)
Hudson	Symons	Lawrence
Doughty	Eliot	Meynell (Mrs.)
Bridges	Bennett	Moore (George)
Hardy	Wells	Dunsany (Lord)

Henry Newbolt (Sir)."

As an afterthought they added: " Rudyard
Kipling and any of Les Jeunes that you like."

I quote the list—after having duly asked per-
mission—and the phrase, because they show fairly well
what Figures the moonshine of our Academe reveals
to the other side of the world. . . . But as for treating
of all these great ones, either seriatim or seriously !
Does the reader remember Wilde's simile of the poor
lion in a den of savage Daniels ?

In what follows you have a line of least resistance :
Reminiscences leading up to a serious plea, the last
being all that this poor *revenant* really cares about.
(But you must put *some* bait in a fox-trap !) The
compiler, then, of the " above Nominal Roll " omits,
surprisingly, the name of Mr. Conrad, and, not surprisingly, that of another writer. Let us begin with
those two—classing them amongst " Les Jeunes that
you like."

*   *   *   *   *

It is, say, twenty-two years and six months since

about Michaelmas, 1897, I received from Mr. Conrad a letter in which, amazingly, he asked me to collaborate with him. He stated that he had consulted W. E. Henley as to his difficulties with English Prose, which were very great since he thought in Polish, expressed his thoughts to himself in French, and, only with great labour, rendered his thus-worded French thoughts into English. Mr. Conrad stated that he had said to Mr. Henley: "Why should I not find as collaborator the finest English Stylist?"... The letter was the result of Henley's advice.

That particular mendacity pleased me—and has ever since pleased me so that I have never asked Mr. Conrad to tell the sober truth of the matter, which was that Henley had never even heard of my existence. For I had a curious row with Henley later —a quite innocent, temporary combat over a slip of the tongue on his part. If I had been less shy and awkward I should not have corrected him. As a parting shot he "squashed" me (people used to squash each other still in those days!) by saying: "Who the H—ll are you, anyway? I never even heard your name!"

Henley was a fine fellow: a crystallised and more vocal specimen of the English peasant who sits in a corner of a settee by the ale-house fire and utters eternal truths. He was diseased and brave as Johnson was diseased and brave. He was wise, as Mr. Hardy and Mr. Hudson are wise amongst the writers of to-day, and—*il faisait école!* He was the revivifying centre to which returned for reinspiration a whole body of English writers. For those of us who live to-day and lived then, he was the first English head

of a group to advocate conscious literary Art, that
elusive marsh-fire that only so very occasionally
shines over the surface of our moonlit pools and
morasses.

You have, that is to say, to go back a hundred
years to find such another, and you will find him in
Samuel Johnson ; you have to go back yet another
hundred and fifty years to find one again—let us say
in Ben Jonson or Lily.

I should like here to make the note that the
literary history of the United States parted company
with the literary history of these Islands forty or
fifty years ago.   Before the 'seventies and 'eighties
you had Hawthorne and Irving; Holmes, Emerson,
and the Concord Group.   They, for better or for
worse, were English Great Writers.   But, with
Daisy Miller, the United States joined itself to the
main literary stream of the world which flows—and
for a hundred years has flowed—through France
alone.

In 1895 or so I bought at a Kentish farm house
sale a great many numbers—sixty or seventy—of the
Atlantic Monthly of the 'seventies and 'eighties.   It
was astonishing to buy these periodicals beneath the
high skies, off the grass of an English farm : heaps
had been thrown down between the coulters of
ploughs and cider tubs on the trodden green turf.
But it astonished me still more to find that correspondent after correspondent had written from Boston,
Mass., and from Philadelphia, Pa., to ask the Editor of
the monthly *how* to write short stories—not merely
what moral attached to this or that example of this
difficult form, but quite simply, " how short stories
should be written."

I had never, in England, heard that question asked. In those far away times the English writer, as I knew him, bothered very much as to what magazines printed short stories ; as to the price per thousand words paid for them ; even as to the respectability of the Short Story as compared with that of the Novel. But as to how the Short Story—or the Long Story, or even the Novel—should be written : never. *Il ne s'en f—t pas mal!*

I think I used to be alone among English-born writers in worrying, in bothering my head, primarily, about the " how " of writing. Henry James did— but he was born in Newport, R.I. ; or Cambridge, Mass. ; or somewhere. Mr. Conrad did—but he was born in the Government of Kief ; used to think in French ; and translate his thoughts with difficulty into English. Mr. Hudson does—and he was born in La Plata, and is of New England stock. Mr. Robert Bontine Cunninghame Graham certainly also does—but he is a Scotch South American—or at any rate spoke Spanish before he spoke English.

I don't mean to say that no other English writers bothered their heads at all about the " how " of writing—merely that during the later 'nineties I personally came across few traces of this pre-occupation. I remember, for instance, listening respectfully to a certain delightful Novelist whilst he lectured me on how to write. But, as far as I could see, his only technical rule was this : *Never introduce your hero and heroine together in the first chapter.* I don't know why this should be so. For the sake of economy, I dare say.*

---

* Whilst these pages were passing through the *English Review*, this gentleman addressed to the Editor of that periodical a letter which will be

This affair, then, represents practically the whole of my personal contact with writers who, before 1900, let us say, had considered the advisability of studying their Art as a painter studies painting or a musician music. Documentarily I might have discovered others. Mr. Arnold Bennett, for instance, very obviously acquired an immense knowledge of " technique " during years spent in Paris. But—I am judging from *The Truth about an Author*—he represents his employment of the pen, at any rate during these years as having been so dominantly commercial that I hesitate to classify his work. And indeed he is able to speak for himself. So much of Mr. Bennett's work, that is to say has been skilfully and consciously written to catch the taste of the moment in provincial Anglo-Saxondom, as distinct from the deeper instincts of a universal humanity that, although I have lately reread almost the whole of this writer's works—as indeed I have reread the complete works of a number of our comtemporaries—for the purpose of

---

found *in extenso* by those who wish to consult it—where it was originally printed. It contains a good deal of personal abuse of myself which can be of no public interest. It concludes thus :

"LITERATURE is not jewellery, it has quite other aims than perfection, and the more one thinks ' how it is done,' the less one gets it done. These critical indulgences lead along a fatal path away from every interest towards a preposterous emptiness of technical effort, a monstrous egotism of artistry, of which the later work of Henry James is the monumental warning. ' It,' the subject, the thing or the thought, has long since disappeared in these amazing works, nothing remains but the way it has been ' manipulated.' No beauty is left, no discovery. Here are no healing waters of thought, no fair gardens of invention, no distant prospects."

This seems to me as able a statement of the objections to my life-long point of view as I could easily—or with difficulty find. I print it here so that the Uninstructed Reader may have my opponents' case well put before him. It gives, in short the point of view of what, later and for convenience, I shall call the Typical English Writer—and Critic.

altering or confirming my present judgments, I cannot formulate very much here. From the first word of Mr. Bennett's that I ever read I have had the feeling that here was the dark horse of comtemporary letters. But, for my immediate purpose it is sufficient to say that Mr. Bennett is a writer very English in temperament who has acquired very great skill from the study, very largely, of French-Russian models. That ought to be the most formidable combination in the world—and perhaps it is !

But, in the middle and late 'nineties, after the collapse of the Yellow Book School and the dispersal of the Henley "gang," I did not even know of Mr. Bennett's existence ; far less could one be expected to know of his technical studies. It was not until well on into the present century that the *Man from the North* was insistently forced into my hands by the writer of the letter just quoted in a note. It was given to me as an instance of extreme technical skill.

And it occurs to me that—from my peculiar point of view—I should be unjust if I omitted to mention the author of the *Villa Rubein*, a very lovely book. One is apt nowadays to let one's remembrance of this earnest student of Turgenev be overwhelmed by the image of the more purposeful sociologist and philanthropist. But it will be obvious to the reader of Mr. Galsworthy's earlier work that this writer made—and indeed, in the 'nineties he did make—a very deep study of Turgenev's frame of mind and so contributed to spreading through Anglo-Saxondom, a taste for the works of the "beautiful genius" of Russia.

And of course I have forgotten Mr. George Moore. One so frequently forgets Mr. Moore that, by force of remembering him with successive shocks he is beginning to occupy a very large space in the shadowy moonlight of one's revisitations. For Mr. Moore is the only consummate English writer (of course he is an Irishman trained by the French). He, alone amongst novelists and writers of the fiction which is called memoirs, knows exactly what he wants to say, and exactly how to say it. But all his fiction repels me : I wish it didn't, I can't help it. Intellectually I am lost in admiration : sympathetically it leaves me cold : or rather, it chills me. But *Ave atque Vale* is beautiful and poetic. . . .

I think, then, that I have said enough to strike the note I want to strike for these pages— that I am interested only in how to write, and that I care nothing—but nothing in the world !— what a man writes about. In the end that is the attitude of every human soul—only they don't know it.

Let us see, then, where this dogmatic statement lands us. For it is a dogmatic statement that almost every English writer will cry out against — and violently. Yet it is so reasonable !

You read Poe—or you read Homer. What do they matter to you—the murders in the Rue de la Morgue, or the dying hound of Ulysses ? Very little ! It is unlikely that you will murder or be murdered ; it is improbable that, ever, your wanderings shall be so protracted that, on your return, your wife will not know you, whereas your nurse will recognise your scarred feet or your blind dog, your odours. Nevertheless you have read the *Gold Bug* and *The Pit and The Pendulum,* and you have read the *Odyssey.* Why?

What is Hecuba to you?

II

WE set out then on our research for the Absolute in Literature. . . .

In those days Mr. Conrad was . . . Conrad. I have never known another writer who on the surface was so exactly his books. Other writers you had to dig into. If you "dug into" Henry James, below many layers of caricaturable oddities—and what finenesses ! —you found *What Maisie Knew*, the *Death of the Lion*, the *Real Thing*—and sometimes even the *Great Good Place*. Beneath the mordant verbal cruelties and polite sneers you might find the George Meredith of *Evan Harrington ;* beneath the kind gentleness of Mr. Thomas Hardy—as the roots of oaks are buried beneath soft grasses and mossy turves —the oaken permanence of this great poet. . . . As for Mr. George Moore. . . .

But Mr. Conrad was always just "Marlow," the reflective, hyper-conscientious narrator of *Youth*, of *Heart of Darkness*, and of *Lord Jim*. I remember Henry James calling Marlow : "This impossible, this monstrous, master-mariner." But then Mr. James used to call me : "Ce jeune homme modeste. . . ."

I don't know that I was modest ; but I suppose I had the sense to be silent before my betters. And life for me, then, was one long alternation of technical riddles : there was Mr. Conrad who, as collaborator, used to tell me that I could not write, never should be able to write, should do better if I did *any*thing other than write. And there was Mr. James! For many years he came to tea nearly every other winter after-noon at my house in Winchelsea, and used to talk in the never-ending sentences—the lovable, glamorous sentences! But I am perfectly certain that he was serenely unaware that I had any literary ambitions. . . .

To finish with that collaboration, then, in a few words! *Romance* was the better known outcome of our labours. And they were labours! It was preceded by another book, the *Inheritors*, which has baffled the comments of even the most inspired of Mr. Conrad's American Press agents. I fancy that neither has any great artistic value—and I am using the history of the joint effort merely as a sort of Observation Car from which to peruse in memory the shadowy literary history of the last quarter century. These glimpses of the moon reveal, more and more, two solitary figures : for the history of definite, conscious, and, as you might say, contagious æsthetic effort during this period became more and more a history of Mr. James and Mr. Conrad and their followers.

In the beginning, again, there were Henley and his school. One remembers of them Stevenson, R. A. M. Stevenson, Mr. Marriott Watson, and George Warrington Steevens—I think Mr. Whibley and Mr. Wedmore also belonged to the Gang. There were no doubt others ; but these were enough to make up a vocal and combative body. They admired physical force, lawlessness, piracy, the speed of motor-cars, the deftness of linotype machines, and they studied words from the Authorised Version and Sir Thomas Browne. They were succeeded, overlappingly, by the Yellow Book School.

That school concerned itself with "form," with the expression of fine shades, with continental models and exact language. It gave a second birth to Henry James, who, after a blaze of popularity which came with *Daisy Miller* and the *American*, had gradually declined through the *Princess Casamassima,* into comparative obscurity and comparative inaction. It— the *Yellow Book*—had for its *chef d'Ecole* Henry Harland, another American of French training; and it included amongst its writers Miss Ethel Colburn Mayne, who only last year published her best work, *Blind Man*.

I should like to make a note of digression here and say a word about Miss Mayne, a great, or, at any rate, a consummate artist. It is indeed my duty to make the digression since the literary history of our Islands would be incomplete without a strongly underlined note about this writer. To-day Miss Mayne stands alone as a portrayer, of the fine shades of civilised contacts—as a portrayer, then, of life as it is lived by you and me. For no one will to-day assert that his life is really an affair of bashings of skulls, plots, conspirings, piracies, of Wall Street panics, debauches, or the improbable rewards of virtue. And no one will deny that his life is really a matter of "affairs"; of minute hourly embarrassments; of sympathetic or unsympathetic personal contacts; of little-marked successes and failures of queer jealousies, of muted terminations—a tenuous, fluttering, and engrossing fabric. And intangible!

And, now that Mr. James is dead, there seems to

remain only Miss Mayne in England who has the perception and the great skill to be the real historian of this our fugitive day. She has, I suppose, no following at all, and not enough readers. That is queer. For, if you write a book about a man's neighbourhood, he and all his neighbours will flock to read it; but if you write about a man's real life he will say that he has to live enough of that during the twenty-four hours of the day, so that he desires to read of Wall Street Pirates by his fireside. . . .

The *Yellow Book*, then, adorned by Miss Mayne, directed by Henry Harland, and providing a new stage for Henry James, dominated the early 'nineties in England. It found imitators, rivals, detractors, disciples, trumpeters; and the whole Movement united the latter pre-Raphaelites—who stridently proclaimed the doctrine of Art for Art's sake, whilst implying that the practice of Art enforced the breach of the seventh commandment—to writers like Miss Mayne who believed that Art impelled you to register life as it is lived.

Between these two schools—though I have again, flagitiously, forgotten to mention Miss Ella D'Arcy as standing alongside Miss Mayne and Mr. James—there existed a whole band of writers like (Mrs.) George Egerton, Hubert Crackanthorpe, and, I fancy, Miss Dolf Wyllarde. These, as it were, translated *comptes rendus* of breaches of several commandments into terms of the life that we used to live. So the crash came.

In the early 'nineties in England, Literature was an affair for the daily papers and for the weekly illustrated journals. Our inkstands, our favourite pens, our porches and our pergolas, were photographed

and reproduced on shiny paper. Our sayings
were chronicled in small paragraphs separated by
asterisks; we had domestics specially trained to ward
off interviewers. But Oscar Wilde was tried and,
through sheer personal imbecility, condemned. (He
was entreated by the British Government to take a
seven o'clock train for Paris, the warrant for his
arrest not being issued till 8.30 p.m. on that fatal
day.) At once the Typical English Writer rushed in
in hordes—and triumphed.

" Art for Art's sake," he said, " ends in Oscarisms,
in warrants, arrests, trials, and the rest of it."
Harland died of consumption; Hubert Crackanthorpe was drowned in the Seine; Aubrey Beardsley
died of consumption; Wilde wrote *De profundis*. . . .

The Typical English Writer—for the *Yellow
Book* was an Irish-Franco-New England affair—
had pursued his course in periodicals like *To-day* and
the *Detroit Free Press*. Mr. Zangwill and Mr.
Barry Pain were appearing in one; Mr. Kipling, Mr.
Frank Harris, and Mr. Harold Frederick, I believe,
in the other. Mr. Edward Garnett had finished
publishing the " Pseudonym Library," and was being
chef d'Ecole for a whole school of writers who produced what is called *Tranchées de la Vie*—slices
cut out of life as a section is cut out of a melon.
This last school had relatively little preoccupation
with Literature as an Art; they had, in revenge, an
immense desire to further the Social Revolution, to
remove Social Injustices, and to point out that Life
was an excruciatingly dull affair. They gave us
George Gissing, Mark Rutherford—and the Russians.
Thus we owe a very great debt to Mr. Garnett. I
don't suppose we shall ever pay it. But let it at least

be put on record that during very dark years, almost alone, he made life possible for a great many earnest and meritorious writers and, almost alone, he gave us Turgenev and Mr. Conrad—not to mention myself.

In those dark days, then, the influence of the *Yellow Book* group disappeared ; the Typical English Writer began, as the total eclipse of the literary moon passed slowly away, to come into his own ; the Typical English critic, part analyst, part preserver of respectable traditions, like Mr. Colvin, Professor Dowden, and my late uncle, William Rossetti, once more advanced towards academic eminence; Mr. Edward Garnett's beneficent labours assumed an aspect more and more subterranean. Mr. Meredith, Mr. Hardy, and Mr. Swinburne, of the Surviving Great, lived each apart on his little hill ; Mr. James took a serene flight of his own, alighting on the battlemented heights of Rye. Writers avoided writers : there remained no perceptible Literary Life in England. Books were written, but the problems of how best to treat a given subject, or how most exactly to render an Affair—these problems were banned and remained undiscussed.

During all those years—for many years that seemed to pass very slowly—Mr. Conrad and I, ostensibly collaborating, discussed nothing else. Buried deep in rural greennesses we used to ask each other how, exactly, such and such an effect of light and shade should be reproduced in very simple words. We read nothing but French : you might say it was Flaubert, Flaubert, Flaubert all the way. Occasionally we should become enthusiastic over a phrase of Stephen Crane's, such as, " the waves were barbarous and abrupt." Occasionally we would go

together and have tea with Henry James at Rye.   I
think that I was most preoccupied with the simple expression of fine shades ; Mr. Conrad's unceasing search
was for a New Form for the Novel, mine for a non-
literary vocabulary.   And I do not believe that there
were in the England of those days any two other
people whose whole minds and whose unceasing
endeavours were so absolutely given to that one
problem of expression between man and man which is
the end of all conscious literary art.   I do not mean
to say that no other writers tried to tell stories well,
or that none told them better ; merely that, as far as
I know, at a time when devotion to exact expression
or to the architectonics of art was regarded either as
folly or as subversive of morality, no two other
writers, functioning together, were consciously and so
exclusively preoccupied with those dangerous topics.

Since that day there have been no Movements in
English Letters—until, just before the war, we had
the Futurists, Vorticists, Imagistes.   The story of
literature became one of individual efforts without
any particularly visible cohesion.   These I leave
aside.

III

WE set out, then, to search for a New Form for the Novel, and, possibly, a formula for the Mot Juste. A modest quest ; but we demanded nothing less.

Since I have said that Mr. Conrad was, of the two, the more preoccupied with the question of form, modesty demands that I should treat of that first—though whether of right contour comes before texture I leave to other pens to decide. Let us ascertain what the author of the *Nigger of the Narcissus* meant when he spoke of a New Form for the English Novel :

Looking around us, then, at our predecessors and contemporaries, and the models they presented to our view, we saw only one thing: the sacrificing—the ignoring indeed—of every other attribute of Art in order to produce the Strong Situation. All characters had to be outlined *à coups de hache*, to be seven feet high and to walk from two to four feet above the ground in order that, towards the end of a book one of them might exclaim : " And my poor fool is dead ! " or another, " Curse you, Copperfield ! " And, indeed, conversing yesterday with one of our most distinguished critics as to the relative values of James and Meredith, I was astonished to hear him say : " Yes : the *Real Thing* is all very well ; but consider the

matchless situation in chapter xvi (or it may have
been xvii) of *Emilia*. That scene alone is worth all
that Henry James ever wrote." He went on to say that
all the rest of *Emilia* bored him—but he repeated
that that one Strong Situation washed out all claims
of the author of the *Princess Casamassima* to be considered alongside the author of *Evan Harrington*.

I bring in those two books on purpose, for in each
the influence of Dickens is enormously evident. It
was, in fact, as difficult for any one born shortly before
1850 to escape the influence of the author of *Little
Dorrit* as it is for all of us, born since 1603, to avoid
that of the authors of *Lear*—and the Authorised
Version. The great passion of humanity—to be
" told fairy tales to "—is undying. Why, indeed,
should it die ? C'est doux ; c'est aimable ; et ca sent
. . . la mère, I suppose. Nevertheless there are
other occupations for grown men. And the novels
of Dickens, Fielding, and Shakespeare are in form
(leaving aside the question of texture) fairy tales for
adults.

At the date of which I am writing—say a quarter
of a century ago—the Novel was still the newest, as
it remains the Cinderella, of Art-Forms. (That of
the " Movies " had not yet appeared.) The practice
of Novel Writing had existed for a bare two hundred
and fifty years : the novelist was still regarded as a
rogue and vagabond, and the Novel as a " waste of
time "—or worse. And the idea of the Novel as a
work of Art, capable of possessing a Form, even as
Sonnets or Sonatas possess Forms—that idea had
only existed since 1850, and in the France of Flaubert
alone, at that. Writers had certainly aimed at
" progressions of effect," in short efforts since the

days of Margaret of Navarre; and obviously what
the Typical English Novelist had always aimed at—
if he had aimed at any Form at all—and what the
Typical English Critic looked for—if ever he con-
descended to look at a Novel—was a series of short
stories with linked characters and possibly a culmination. Indeed, that conception of the Novel has
been forced upon the English Novelist by the
commercial exigencies of hundreds of years. The
Romances of Shakespeare, novels written for ranted
recitation and admirable in the technique of that
Form, were moulded by the necessity for concurrent
action in varying places: the curtain had to be used.
So you had the Strong Situation in order that the
psychological stages of Othello should be firm in the
hearer's mind whilst Desdemona was alone before the
audience. The Novels of Fielding, of Dickens, and of
Thackeray were written for publication in Parts: at
the end of every part must come the Strong Situation,
to keep the Plot in the reader's head until the First
of Next Month. So with the eminent contemporaries
of ours in the 'nineties of last century: if the writer
was to make a living wage he must aim at Serialisation:
for that once again you must have a Strong Scene
before you write " To be continued," or the reader
would not hanker for the next number of the magazine you served. But you do not need to go to
Commercial Fiction to find the origin of the tendency:
if the reader has ever lain awake in a long school
dormitory or a well-peopled children's bedroom,
listening to or telling long, long tales that went on
from day to day or from week to week, he will have
known, or will have observed, the necessity to retain
the story in the hearer's mind, and to introduce, just

before each listener's head sank on the pillow—the
Strong Situation. Indeed, Scheherezade knew that
pressing need !

It was against the tyranny of this convention that
Mr. Conrad was revolting when so passionately he
sought for the New Form. How often, in those
distant days, lamenting the unlikelihood of our making
even modest livings by our pens, have we not sigh-
ingly acknowledged that Serialisation was not for us !
For I think we both started out with at least this
much of a New Form in our heads : we considered a
Novel to be a rendering of an Affair. We used to
say, I will admit, that a Subject must be seized by
the throat until the last drop of dramatic possibility
was squeezed out of it. I suppose we had to concede
that much to the Cult of the Strong Situation.
Nevertheless, a Novel was the rendering of an Affair :
of one embroilment, one set of embarrassments, one
human coil, one psychological progression. From
this the Novel got its Unity. No doubt it might
have its cæsura—or even several ; but these must be
brought about by temperamental pauses, markings of
time when the treatment called for them. But the
whole novel was to be an exhaustion of aspects, was
to proceed to one culmination, to reveal once and for
all, in the last sentence, or the penultimate ; in the
last phrase, or the one before it—the psychological
significance of the whole. (Of course, you might
have what is called in music your Coda.) But it is
perfectly obvious that such a treatment of an Affair
could not cut itself up into Strong Situations at the
end of every four or every seven thousand words.
That market, at least, was closed to us.

I have suggested that we were more alone in our

search for the New Form than, very likely, we
actually were. (There was, of course, always Mr.
George Moore.) Mr. Bennett must, at that date,
have been engaged in acquiring the immense knowledge of French tricks and devices that his work has
since displayed. But I fancy he had as little love for
pure Form for its own sake as he has for the French.
I may be wrong. I have also—quite impenitently—
misrepresented another eminent Novelist when, on a
former page, I stated that he lectured me on one
æsthetic form—that which prohibited the introduction
of the hero and heroine in the first chapter. It went,
naturally, further than that.

Certainly he lectured. Being the one more avid
of life and sensation, he would. Indeed, almost
everybody I have ever come across has lectured me—
from Mr. Holman Hunt to Mr. Pound. Nevertheless, during the lecture I pursued what I will call
subconscious cogitation. It was, I suppose, in 1899
or thereabouts, and at last I got my word in, somewhat as follows :—

SELF. I suppose then, in the matter of Form, you arrive at
     the Sonata.

E. N. Yes, that's it. What *is* the Sonata?

SELF. Like this: You state your first subject (Hero or
     Heroine) in the key of the Tonic. You then state
     your second subject (Heroine or Hero) in the key of
     the Dominant, if the first subject is in a major—or
     in the key of the relative major, if the first subject
     is in a minor key. You repeat all that, and that
     finishes the first part. Then comes what is called the
     working out or Free Fantasia. . . .

E. N. Then there is some Freedom. . . .

SELF. In that you mix up themes A and B, embroider on

them in any related, or even unrelated, keys and
tempi. You introduce foreign matter if you like. . . .

E. N. I see. The Tertium, what is it?

SELF. You introduce foreign matter, and generally have a
good time. In the Restatement you restate: A
emphatically in his or her key, and B, equally
emphatically, but in the tonic original key of A.
That becomes the key of the whole Sonata: Op.
232 in E Flat Major! You *might* restate the
Foreign Matter which you introduced in the Free
Fantasia. . . .

E. N. Ah!

SELF. But that is irregular. And you may or may not have
a Coda, a short sweet passage of reminiscence—the
children tumbling over the Newfoundland on the
lawn.

E. N. Don't you mean the feeling of relief after the divorce?

SELF. Of course, the Coda should give a feeling of relief.

E. N. To think of you knowing all that. I thought you were
only interested in Golf!

In the meantime, magisterially and at leisure, in
Rye, Henry James was performing the miracles after
whose secrets we were merely groping. I don't
know why—but we rather ignored that fact. For,
in the end, Mr. Conrad found salvation not in any
machined Form, but in the sheer attempt to reproduce in words life, as it presents itself to the intelligent
observer. I daresay, if we could only perceive it,
Life has a pattern. I don't mean that of birth,
apogee, and death, but a woven symbolism of its
own. The Pattern in the Carpet, Henry James
called it—and that he saw something of the sort was
no doubt the secret of his magic. But, though I
walked with and listened to the Master day after
day, I remember only one occasion on which he

made a remark that was a revelation of his own aims and methods. That I will reserve until it falls in place in the pattern of my own immediate carpet. For the rest, our intercourse resolved itself into my listening silently and wondering unceasingly at his observation of the littlest things of life.

"Are you acquainted," he would begin, as we strolled under the gateway down Winchelsea Hill towards Rye. . . . Ellen Terry would wave a gracious hand from her garden above the old Tower, and the leash of Maximilian would require several readjustments, and the dog himself a great many sotto voce admonitions as to his expensive habit of chasing sheep into dykes. "Are you acquainted," the Master would begin again, "with the terrible words . . ."

A higgler, driving a cart burdened with crates of live poultry, would pass us. The Master would drive the point of his cane into the roadway. "Now *that* man!" he would exclaim. And he would break off to say what hideous, what appalling, what bewildering, what engrossing, Affairs were going on all round us in the little white cottages and farms that we could see, dotting Playden Hill and the Marsh to the verge of the great horizon. "Terrible things!" he would say. "Appalling! . . . Now that man who just passed us. . . ." And then he would dig his stick into the road again and hurry forward, like the White Queen escaping from disaster, dropping over his shoulder the words; "But that probably would not interest you. . . ."

I don't know what he thought *would* interest me!

So he would finish his sentence before the door above the high steps of Lamb House:

" Are you acquainted with the terrible, the devastating words, if I may call them so, the fiat of Doom: 'I don't know if you know, sir'? As when the housemaid comes into your bedroom in the morning and says: 'I don't know if you know, sir, that the bath has fallen through the kitchen ceiling!'"

My own servants used to say that his eyes looked you through and through until you could feel your own backbone within you, and it was held in Rye that he practised black magic behind the high walls of Lamb House. . . .

IV

I HAVE said that I remember only one occasion on which Henry James spoke of his own work. That was like this: He had published the *Sacred Fount,* and was walking along beside the little shipyard at the foot of Rye Hill. Suddenly he said:

"You understand. . . . I *wanted* to write the *Great Good Place* and the *Altar of the Dead.* . . . There are things one wants to write all one's life, but one's artist's conscience prevents one. . . . And then . . . perhaps one allows oneself. . . ."

I don't know what he meant. . . . Or I do! For there *are* things one wants to write all one's life—only one's artist's conscience prevents one. That is the first—or the final, bitter—lesson that the Artist has to learn: that he is not a man to be swayed by the hopes, fears, consummations or despairs of a man. He is a sensitised instrument, recording to the measure of the light vouchsafed him what is—what *may* be—the Truth. I fancy that that is why the idea of applying any theory of art to the process of writing is so disliked by the typical English Man of Letters. . . . We are such a nation of Individualists. For I assure you it was hated—that idea; it was hunted; it was cried down—as if, in advocating the research for Form in a Novel or the just word in a

49

phrase, you were not only advocating an unnatural vice or practising a hypocrisy, but as if you were likely to cause certain pecuniary loss to any one who followed, or even so much as listened to, that *hærœsia damnosa!* How often have I not read sentences like these which come back to me from a ten-year-old review in the *Daily Telegraph*.

"Thank Heavens, we have outgrown the stage when English novelists bother their heads about the phraseology and the shape of their fiction. Mr. —— writes a straightforward, rattling tale in straightforward language. . . ."

The novelist—I forget his name—had, in fact, "selected an excellent subject and treated it in a very spirited manner." [That was Henry James's wonderful, sardonic politeness: he addressed it to novelists who sent him books he did not care for.] The work (I now remember the work) may have caused the Author some intellectual struggles. The reading called for none. I want to talk, however, of the "phraseology."

This Author, then (*Please:* he was a modest, unaffected English gentleman—I never in my life grudged him anything that his simple, honest novels brought him in—the desirable country place, the charming wife, the sons at Harrow. Nothing have I ever grudged him!) This Author, then, had been educated at Harrow and Oxford. In consequence his "style" for pedestrian passages of narrative was that of the daily organ with the better type of social circulation. For descriptive passages he used the phraseology of Shakespeare, as it is found in the pages of Charles Lamb. He was fond of innocent quotations; when describing starlight he would talk of patines of bright gold. For his emotional passages, strong situations, or tragic moments—these, of course, were very rare in his works!—he and his characters had recourse to the " phraseology " and the Cadences of the Authorised Version or the Book of Common Prayer. So that if the hero went anywhere he hailed a hansom or repaired to his tailor: but, if a ship took fire at sea, the conflagration illumined the heavens, and the heroine said, " Intreat me not to leave thee or to leave off from following after thee." . . . A kindly and simple soul was here revealed.

Between that, then, and the "interjected finger" of Stevenson that "delayed the action of the time-piece" (and, for the matter of that, the stretched forefinger of Old Time that, I suppose, must go on sparkling for ever), we set out to search for a formula for the *Mot Juste*. Let me now particularise with great care, for, if I do not get this clear, all is indeed lost. This was how the world presented itself to our eyes: On the one hand, we had the respectable journal, critic and author whose desire was to make a not difficult living. On the other side of the fence were those literary alchemists who aim at attaining immortality by means of jewels five words long. The respectable journal could not wish to be forced to use any more actual verbiage than the *cliché phrase*—the phrase that has been mumbled so over and over by tired jaws that you can write it half asleep and "peruse" it without disturbance during the degusta-tion of your post-prandial port. Speakers according to this dialect are always cordially received; they do not anticipate a large exodus of Jews to Palestine; they oppose one thing or another on the grounds that the proposals are novel and of a far-reaching character. And their hansoms always have to be hailed. The Critics and supporters of these Respectabilia did not object to the fabricators of the jewels five words long, because when such a jewel has been a jewel for long enough, it can be imported into diurnal columns and be hallowed as a *cliché*. But they *did* object—and very wildly—to *le mot juste*. It was something foreign; it was indescribably troublesome. You had, they said, the "sound English" in which the daily, weekly, monthly, and quarterly periodicals are still written. You had also Fine Writing—to be used occasionally. That meant fourteen words, or forty, or half a page, of tired prose and then a shot at a five-word jewel. That was easy. But—so it seemed to them—*le mot juste* meant "every word a sparkler." That was a conception that appalled our friends. It subverted the ca' canny ideal; it was contrary to the rules of the Best of Trade Unions; it was a product of snuffly, foreign, affected or sexually perverted minds. Alas! for that miserable literary botcher who—as I once heard a French Critic say—*péchait par pur snobisme*.

The trouble, however, with us was this: we could not get our own prose keyed down enough. We wanted to write, I suppose, as only Mr. W. H. Hudson writes—as simply as the grass grows. We desired to achieve a style—the *habit* of a style—so simple that you would notice it no more than you notice the unostentatious covering of the South Downs. The turf has to be there, or the earth would not be green.

Our most constant preoccupation, then, was to avoid words that stuck out of sentences either by their brilliant unusualness or their "amazing aptness."

For either sort of word arrests the attention of a
reader, and thus "hangs up" both the meaning and
the cadence of a phrase. We wanted the Reader to
forget the Writer—to forget that he was reading.
We wished him to be hypnotised into thinking that
he was living what he read—or, at least, into the
conviction that he was listening to a simple and in no
way brilliant narrator who was telling—not writing—
a true story. Mind you, that was not easy : it was perhaps easier for me than for Mr. Conrad ; or perhaps it
would be more just to say that I desired it more than
Mr. Conrad did. For, by sheer reaction of inheritance,
I had even then an absolute hatred for the "toll-loll"
Great Figure, the Quarterly Reviewer, the Biblio-
grapher, and the ceaselessly mouthing Great Poet,
who had overshadowed my childhood. Such disadvantages Mr. Conrad had not known, so that he
had less of my hatred for Fine Writing : but his difficulties were greater. He was conquering—conquering,
truly—a foreign language. And that language was
particularly unsuited to our joint purpose, in that its
more polite forms, through centuries of literary
usage, have become absolutely unsuited to direct
statement. You cannot make a direct statement in
Literary English. And Mr. Conrad came to it by
way of Miss Braddon and the English Bible. . . .

In the end, of course, he achieved both a Form
and a habit of language : he invented the figure of
Marlow. To Henry James, whose eye for other
people's work was, strangely, too literary, Marlow
was always a fabulous Master Mariner. James
refused to believe in him any more than he would
believe in any other mechanical device. It was
useless to argue with him : he used to groan over the

matter and, if I persisted at all, would end by saying that Mr. Conrad—or Marlow, that old Man of the Sea, that incredible but enduring Vampire—was ruining my prospects.

He was wrong. Marlow is a natural, simple and not at all unusual, peasant type. He is wise as to human vicissitudes, as the simple or the merely poor are so frequently wise: but he is not over-read in the book-lore that is so inevitably destructive of wisdom. If I go up the hill from where I sit, on the fifty-foot contour line, or thereabouts, I shall find an old shepherd. He will be just as wise as Marlow. And, gradually, from this old man I am learning the history of a fabulous farmer, Mr. Cummings. I know already that in 1892 Mr. Cummings married his third wife. Till 1870 he still bred the old, horned, Wiltshire sheep that has now disappeared. About 1880 he ate five-pound notes between thin bread and butter—to annoy the Income Tax Authorities. In 1879 he married the first Mrs. Cummings; she was still living when he married No. II. and No. III. Apparently all three ladies lived together in the great old farm till 1900. He was a little, terrible, swearing man, with a pimply face and no teeth. He was the first man to use a steam-plough in these parts, and his eldest son went to America because he didn't hold with it. That would be about 1894. In 1869 Annie Meggott drowned herself in the Arun: Mr. Cummings never got over that. It was why he was like what he was. For, in 1902, on his deathbed, he sent for the old shepherd and said: "That Annie Meggott she was terrible pernickety. But upstanding and with red cheeks." He had lost the use of one eye by then.

You perceive that that is how Marlow gets hold of and tells the stories of exceptional men. And it is in that way that life really presents itself to us: not as a rattling narrative beginning at a hero's birth and progressing to his not very carefully machined yet predestined glory—but dallying backwards and forwards, now in 1890, now in 1869 ; in 1902—and then again in 1869—as forgotten episodes came up in the minds of simple narrators. And, if you put your Affair into the mouth of such a narrator your phraseology will be the Real thing in *mots justes*, for just so long as they remain within his probable vocabulary. There will be no jewels five words long, nor, for that matter, will the narrator say that Mr. Cummings ever hailed a hansom.

V

AFTER a great many years of studious seclusion, one
of us at least having found his Form—and no doubt
also a haven—the day came for a voyage into the
Great World of English Letters. This World was
beginning timidly to reconquer a little of moonlit
glory—of Parnassian opulence. When I look again
at the lists provided for me by my Trans-atlantic
taskmaster, I perceive the names of few eminent men
who were not already well in the saddle at the close
of the first decade of this century. Let us just repeat
the list to save the Reader the trouble of turning
back. You have then :

(Messrs.)		
Gosse	Yeats	Sinclair (Miss)
Hudson (W. H.)	Symons	Lawrence (D. H.)
Doughty	Eliot (T. S.)	Meynell (Mrs.)
Bridges	Bennett	Moore (George)
Hardy	Wells	Dunsany (Lord)
	Newbolt, Sir Henry	

and, the Reader may remember that the compiler
added : " Rudyard Kipling and any of Les Jeunes "
—that I liked. Alas ! I liked them all !

If we add the names of George Meredith and
Henry James, who were then still alive and that of
Mr. Conrad ; and, if we omit those of Messrs. Eliot

and Lawrence, neither of whom had yet begun to write, we shall have a fairly representative gathering of those who in the moonlight occupied thrones, or at least seats on the steps of England's Parnassus during the years 1907, 8 and 9. It makes, this list, a distinguished and varied array, and heaven forbid that one should presume to criticise its individual members. It wants only one thing—cohesion.

You can't imagine its units uniting for any imaginable purpose—except perhaps pontifically to proscribe Conscious Literary Artists. Even then there would be one or two dissentients. I, on the other hand, couldn't in those days imagine Literature without, behind it, some cohesion of writers. The poor old *métier de chien* is such a solitary business; without some contagion to sustain his belief in himself a writer can do so little. And the usual contagion supplied to the Eminent Littérateur of England, sitting solitary on the little hill that he makes his own—the contagion supplied by his body-servant, his bottle-washer, his solicitor and several female admirers, is a poor substitute for the sharpening of wits that must take place when many rivals—as in the Mermaid—meet habitually and talk about how to write. The poor dear old Pre-Raphaelite Brotherhood, the great Flaubert-Turgenev-Zola-Maupassant-Goncourt group, the "Henley Gang," as it called itself, and the *Yellow Book*—each of these movements did something towards providing a solution for one problem or another in Art, or towards proving the futility of one method or another. And, if each did no more than prove that a little generosity is possible amongst men who sometimes hold pens, each did a great deal.

In the lightness of our hearts and the inexperience of early middle age, Arthur Pearson Marwood—alas, that I must write: the late!—and myself set out to afford a nucleus for some sort of Movement that should combine some of the already Eminent * with some of the Young who were then knocking on the doors of our Athenæum. It was in one of the three years I have mentioned: I have really forgotten which: and it does not matter. We aimed at founding an *aube de siècle* Yellow Book. We did— or perhaps we didn't!

At any rate, when I look again through that list of names I see only those of four gentlemen who did not write for us; of these, Mr. Kipling was omitted because we could not pay his prices; the others we did not like. Yet—I am talking about cohesion—of all the writers who contributed to our first three or four numbers there was hardly one who did not write to us to say that the *English Review* was ruined by the inclusion of every other contributor. Mr. James, curiously enough, said: " Poor dear old Meredith—God alone knows what he *means!* " Mr. Meredith said: " Poor James is ageing. . . . He has these mysterious internal rumblings. But what do they *mean?* " One own familiar literary friend of Marwood and myself wrote us a full-dress letter of remonstrance. He pointed out that we were " ruin- ing our careers " by " having anything to do with " Mr. Bennett, Mr. Hardy, Mr. Hudson, Mr. James,

---

* Mr. Monro in his book on Twentieth Century poets reminds me that we founded the *English Review* in order to print a poem by Mr. Hardy— the *Sunday Morning Tragedy*. It is a literal fact that our indignation that this great poem should have been refused publication by one of the then orthodox periodicals finally spurred us to set out on a troublesome venture. Till that date we had only discussed it rather vaguely.

Mr. Meredith, Mr. Wells, or Mr. Yeats. . . . *Cela vous donne une fière idée de l'homme!*

And, really, it was a mad idea we had had— that part of the enterprise that attempted to cement together the Immortals. " The books are alive to this day to testify to it, therefore deny it not." We fell back in the end altogether on *Les Jeunes*, and Les Jeunes made a very pretty movement for themselves, only the war cut it short. Les Jeunes, as they chronologically presented themselves to us, were Mr. Pound, Mr. D. H. Lawrence, Mr. Norman Douglas, Mr. Flint, " H. D.," Mr. Richard Aldington, Mr. T. S. Eliot—I daresay I am forgetting somebody ; he or she must forgive it.

But I wish to be allowed to break off once again to pay a tribute to the memory of the late Arthur Marwood. He was too unambitious to be a writer but, large, fair, clumsy, and gentle, he had the deepest and widest intelligence of all the men I have ever met. He had the largest general, the largest encyclopædic, knowledge that, I imagine, it would be possible for any one man's skull to hold. He could discourse, and accurately, about the rigging of fruit schooners, about the rotation of crops on sandy soils, about the home life of Ammianus Marcellinus, the vocabulary of Walter Pater, the hidden aims of Mr. Chamberlain, systems of irrigation, the theories of Mendel, the rapture of Higher Mathematics, Napoleonic strategy, consubstantiation, or the Theory of Waves. . . . Why he ever had anything to do with the *English Review* I do not know. He had no personal ambitions, being a Yorkshire Tory Squire, a distinguished mathematician and the Fellow of some Cambridge College—Trinity, I think. I can only imagine that

Destiny, who is merciless, blind, and avenging, drove him into that enterprise to punish him for some sin unknown to the rest of the world. And, if the enterprise did not ruin him as our friend had so forcibly predicted, it certainly inconvenienced him and caused him to endure a great deal of mental uneasiness and semi-public odium.

Its only outcome, as a Movement-producer, was the group which figured from 1910 to 1914 as Les Jeunes of London literary life. We printed the " first efforts " of the gentlemen I have just named : I daresay we printed those of other Futurists, Vorticists, Cubists, Imagistes. . . . And, in our Editorial Salons they found chaises-longues and sofas on which to stretch themselves whilst they discussed the fate of already fermenting Europe. So, for three or four years, culminating in the London Season of 1914, they made a great deal of noise in a city that was preparing to reverberate with echoes of blasts still greater. They found their earthly home and general headquarters in a polychromatic and stifling cellar beneath the New Gallery. There—*au son de fiffres de crotale !*—they plotted the blowing of Parnassus to the moon. They came near to doing it. They stood for the Non-Representational in the Arts ; for *Vers Libre ;* for symbols in Prose, *tapage* in Life, and Death to Impressionism. They were a fine band, and did useful work. The war is said to have extinguished them—as if the Germans' invasion of Belgium saved their Parnassian Allies. I wonder if it has.

We now skip five years during which the moon did not much shine—or, at any rate, the denizens of our Parnassus used, I understand, to pray that it would not.

VI

CODA . . .

I WRITE this section—in which at last I come to re-visiting—with great diffidence. I should not write it at all had I not been " put right " by a very young man already eminent in the after-war world of letters. I could have deduced the conditions as to which he dogmatically informs me, as a Scientist deduces the Ichthyosaurus from the long-deceased beast's little-toe joint—but I did not want to deduce a world to me so naked and forlorn. In short, according to my confident and business-like Informer, himself an able Parnassian of the Parnassians, Academicism is now triumphant in these Islands as it never was before. To secure so much as publication you must bow to some image or another of Minerva ; to be reviewed at all you must subscribe to some Fifty Articles ; to be reviewed favourably you must kiss some gentleman's great toe. Mr. Pound, I am told, is dead. Mr. Wadsworth, I think, amongst the Immortals of Burlington House ; Futurism is a byword ; Vers Libristes have all been put into decasyllabic strait-waistcoats ; all the Imagistes are in the workhouse. . . . I wonder, forlornly, what has become of Impressionism. The Futurists killed that, so they used to say in 1914, at the same time telling me negligently that *I* was an Impressionist.

There would be nothing sad about all this if it is not true that the ruling young have become Academic. That would be the most tragic aftermath of the war. To the war went all that was *tapageur*, careless, and uncalculating of Les Jeunes : to the war went the Futurists, the Cubists, the Imagistes, the Vorticists— even the poor old Impressionists. The Eminent Middle-Aged remained in undisturbed possession of the fauteuils of Parnassus ; and, according to my informant, first the door-knockers, and then the steps of the Fane were taken possession of by a serried phalanx of metricists, prosodists, young annalists, young commentators. And there they still remain, controlling all the Sources of Information. That was inevitable : so it was in Athens of old ; so it will be for ever.

But I hope a public-spirited man or two will arise to give the real young a chance. I know that they need it more than at any time in my experience. There may or may not be a Censorship established by the Neo-Academics. I am so triumphantly assured of its existence and powers by one claiming to be on the Board that I must needs believe it. But, apart from that, the mere economics of to-day make it extremely difficult for a young writer even to get his first book printed. Paper is very expensive, binding is very expensive, printing is very expensive, ware-house room is very expensive and difficult to obtain. Initiative on the part of publishers is almost pro-hibited. I don't know that we ought to blame them ; perhaps we ought, but I am not minded to throw the first stone. For we have to blame first the intense but reasonable indifference of the public, the want of conscience of the Reviewers—and, apparently, my young friend and his fellow-censors. If these three could be whipped into mending their ways, the publishers would soon dance to the New Tune.

Reaction towards Academicism is normal to all ages and to most countries. That is decreed by blind and august Destiny. I can't see why it is so decreed, though we all know how it comes about. The Reader will know. He too was once young, careless, *tapageur*, full-blooded; but his waist has grown; he needs a nice country house: he desires to send his sons to Harrow. So he seeks to drive all the younger cockerels off his dunghill. A novelist *de mes amis* to whom I announced my farewell to Letters said: " I'm sorry to hear it, of course. At the same time, it means that I can afford another lump of sugar to my tea." It is, in short, decreed that we should grow towards middle age and wear our laurel with a difference. Usually the young have a fair chance to dig our graves.

To-day they have none—and that is a very serious affair for the world, and for ourselves. We, as a Nation, are too inclined always to be insular and commercial, and a Nation that becomes over-materialist in its aims and over-insular in its views is destined to decay—or to obliteration. We have lately escaped by the skins of our teeth: but we have had an object-lesson. And the politics of Parnassus are no merely domestic wrangles. Stodginess and Academicism at the fount of a nation's intellect mean tenfold Materialism in the race that is content to endure them. A Movement in the Arts—*any* move-ment—leavens a whole Nation with astonishing rapidity: its ideas pour through the daily, the weekly, and the monthly press with the rapidity of water pouring through interstices until at last they reach the Quarterlies and disturb even the Academicians asleep over their paper-baskets. A solitary thinker will take two æons to make his voice heard : seven working in concert will forty-nine times shorten the process. And Movements make for friendships, enthusiasms, self-sacrifice, mutual aid—all fine things ! And Movements are things of youth. I should like to permit myself to write with some emotion of these matters, since they are those I have felt most deeply all my life. But I am aware that emotionalism is inadvisable. The Board of Censors is on the watch for a stumble or a generous over-statement. Let us then take a guarded view of where we stand. I fancy that, when he stated that Mr. Pound was dead ; Mr. Wadsworth an R.A. ; Mr. T. S. Eliot a Wall Street operator, and Mr. Lawrence a whole-time librarian— when, in short, he reported that the whole battalion of Les Jeunes of 1914 had been wiped out, my young friend was reporting as accomplished facts what he had tried to bring about. That is what Censorships do. It is what they are for : thus they encourage recruiting. Mr. Flint and Mr. Pound I know to be alive, and " H.D." and Mr. Aldington of the original Imagistes. So some of Les Jeunes survive : it is not an immense list, but it gives us a nucleus of people who can be trusted to be decent to the young. There is also Mr. James Joyce ; and there is Miss Richardson.

I am inclined to think that Mr. Joyce is riding his method to death. But it is a good thing to ride a method to death : it lets other artists see of what it is capable. And nothing is more useful to the Arts than to be afforded an object-lesson in how far a

Method can be made to go. Mr. Joyce descends
from Mr. James in his perception of minute embarrassments and related frames of mind, and he has
carried Mr. Conrad's early researches after ramified
Form almost as far as they can go. But he is direct
in his narration of incident. This Miss Richardson
isn't. She records incident so unceasingly through
the medium of embarrassments—and so minutely—
that at times one has a difficulty in following her.
But then one is tired, and she has a great following
of ladies.

Women, indeed, seem to have assumed a large
share of the responsibility for carrying forward the
Arts whilst their menfolk were at Cannæ—or was it
Thermopylæ? I am aware, even in my remoteness
—indeed, in a remoteness still greater from the
glimpses of the moon I was aware—of Miss Clemence
Dane, who has worked out a great deal of the method
of Henry James; of Mrs. Virginia Woolf, who has
made a formidable attempt to revive the Standard
Type of English novel; of Miss Stern, who analyses
modern trends of thought and of feminism. And I
should like to put in a special plea for Miss, or Mrs.
George Stevenson, whose book *Benjy*, in a rather
down-to-the-ground style, such as Mr. Garnett tried
to make popular in the 'nineties, I have enjoyed and
reread, as we used to do with the books of our
childhood. So that there, firmly in the saddle, we
have lady representatives of the four schools that
were found in the 'nineties. They carry on, these
ladies, fine traditions—but I doubt if they would
really join either Movements or Revolts, or yet knock
on doors of Parnassian fanes. Perhaps Miss Stern
would, for I take her to represent the *Yellow Book*.

I believe we could count on Miss Sinclair—possibly Miss Mayne, too, still holds Revolutionary fires. And that alone really interests me.

I can't help it. I wish my nature would let me sit, if not beside, then at the feet of the Editors of the more Academic Reviews—or even at the feet of the Academic young who have established claims to the mantles of those others—the bibliophiles, commentators, and Vorschungen-Wallahs. But cheerfulness will come creeping in : one's face will not compose itself to the necessary portentousness. Besides, I have lately had sent me several very striking manuscripts of Young People who cannot find publishers. That is hateful.

And so we come back to the plea with which, letting the cloven hoof at last peep through, I started this chapter : I wish that a public-spirited man or two could be found to throw away a couple of thousand pounds each—to be ready to lose that amount in order to start a Movement. Any Movement! A dead loss of a couple of thousand pounds may represent an amazing stretch of activities, just as the same sum in profit may be all that results from a huge Trade turnover. The Academic and the Indifferent will tell you that that is subsidising Art, and that good Art can only result from what is called a sound commercial line. That is not true. In this country all good art movements have had to be subsidised by original losers—Pre-Raphaelites, Æsthetes, the Henley Gang, the Yellow Book Group. *Atque ego in Arcadia!* . . .

And I ask the Reader to observe that I am not seeking to promote the interests of any one School or Group. I am not even asking any one to give Mr.

Aldington, Mr. Flint, or Captain Read, or any other of the gallant young fellows, what is called in military language a sporting chance to make up the ground that they lost by their periods of Army service. Indeed, the majority of the manuscripts which have lately been sent me have been by Young People of Pacifist Tendencies. That is all one. I simply want to point out that the healthy young are wise with a queer, instinctive wisdom that must be voiced if the Nation is to be kept healthy. They are no doubt also foolish : perhaps they need handicapping.

But to-day the handicap is unjust. The economics of paper and print are *too* strong against them ; the Academic are *too* strongly entrenched against them : they lost too many, of All Ranks, and the nerves of too many others suffered too much in the fields of France and Flanders—or, if you will, on Dartmoor. It is so hopeless playing against unreasonably loaded dice when, for many years, you have suffered a great deal ! They *should* be given a chance. . . .

But I have let emotion creep in.

VII

W. H. HUDSON AND THE SIMPLE WORD

For a long, long time, I daresay for twenty-five years—I have been longing to say something about Mr. Hudson. But what is there to say ? Of things immense, tranquil or consummate, it is difficult indeed to speak or to write. The words are at the tip of the tongue; the ideas at the back of the brain . . . and yet : Nothing! So one says, "immense," "tranquil," "consummate."

Suppose one should say that one would willingly cancel every one of the forty or so books that one has published if one could be given the power to write one paragraph as this great poet writes a paragraph : or that one would willingly give up all one's powers of visualising this and that if one could be granted this great naturalist's power of looking at a little bird. . . . But of course that would not be enough. Or rather it would be nothing at all. For I suppose that if one had the power to frame one paragraph one could frame others : and if one had the vision of the poet one would be the poet's self. One might say—and indeed I do say with perfect sincerity—that one would willingly sacrifice all one's gifts as a writer if one could give to this unapproached master of English ten years longer of writing life. . . . But even that would be selfish—for one would have the pleasure : one would read what he wrote.

For me, then, Mr. Hudson is the unapproached master of the English tongue. There are no doubt other English writers, though English as a language is woefully lacking in prose towards which one need not be kind—in unassailable prose. Still there are possibly other English writers. But there is no other English writer that you cannot say something about. One derives from Sir Thomas Browne—but is not as good ; another gets his effects from a profound study of the Authorised Version but falls short of the resonance of the Inspired Original ; another has caught the jolly humour of Rabelais; when Mr. Peskith writes you might swear it was Montaigne speaking ; some one else puts down the thoughts of Dante in the language of Shakespeare. . . .

As I have said, the only English writer with whom I ever had the luck constantly to discuss the " how " of writing was Mr. Conrad. (I *will* say this for Americans that, if they practise letters, they are much more usually devoured by curiosity about what is called " technique." I have heard Mr. Owen Wister talk for quite a time on several occasions with Mr. James about the written word as a means of expression. I have talked for hours with members of the editorial staff of New York magazines—as to how to write a short story !—and I used to listen for hours whilst Stephen Crane—why is poor dear " Stevie " forgotten ? —talked just about words ! And Crane made the most illuminating remark about English prose that I ever heard.)

And, once, Mr. Conrad looked up from reading *Green Mansions* and said : " You can't tell how this fellow gets his effects ! " And, a long time after I had agreed that I couldn't tell how Mr. Hudson got

his effects, Mr. Conrad continued : " He writes as
the grass grows. The Good God makes it be there.
And that is all there is to it ! " *!*

And there is all there is to it. *Green Mansions*
is the only English novel of passion ; the *Purple Land*
is the only English novel of Romance (and I don't
except Mr. Conrad's and my own Romance), *Nature
in Downland, Hampshire Days, Birds in a Village,*
and the *Shepherd's Life* are the only English books
about England. And you must remember that Mr.
Hudson is an American of New England stock.

I suppose that the chief characteristic of great
writers—of writers who are great by temperament as
well as by industry or contrivance—is self-abandon-
ment. You imagine Mr. Hudson watching a tiny
being and his whole mind goes into the watching :
then his whole mind goes into the rendering.
Probably there is some delight in the watching and
more austerity, more diligence, in the act of recording. That no doubt varies. Turgenev is such
another as Mr. Hudson and I can recall no third.

Turgenev, I mean, watched humanity with much
such another engrossment as Mr. Hudson devotes to
kingfishers, sheep, or the grass of fields and rendered
his results with the same tranquillity. Probably,
however, Turgenev had a greater self-consciousness
in the act of writing : for of Mr. Hudson you might
as well say that he never had read a book. The
Good God makes his words be there. . . . Still, in
the *Sportsman's Sketches*, in the *Singers*, the *Rattle of
the Wheels*, and in *Bielshin Prairie* above all—you get
that note :—of the enamoured, of the rapt, watcher ;
so enamoured and so rapt that the watcher disappears,
becoming merely part of the surrounding atmosphere

amidst which, with no self-consciousness, the men, the forests or the birds act and interact. I know, however, of no other writers that possess this complete selflessness.

It is no doubt this faculty that gives to Mr. Hudson's work the power to suggest vast, very tranquil space and a man absolutely at home in it, or motionless vegetation, a huge forest and a traveller who wishes to go nowhere, nor ever to reach the forest bounds. For you can suggest immensity in your rendering of the smallest of British birds if you know an immense deal about the bird itself; if you have watched innumerable similar birds, travelling over shires, countries, duchies, kingdoms, hemispheres —and always selflessly. So the rendering of one individual bird will connote to the mind of your reader—if you happen to be Mr. Hudson !—the great distances of country in which you have travelled in order that, having seen so many such birds, you may so perfectly describe this one. Great plains will rise up before your reader's mind : immensely high skies; distant blue ranges, woodlands a long way off. . . .

II

It is twenty-five—or twenty-four, or twenty-three !—years ago since I sat with Mr. Conrad, one day in the drawing-room of my farm-house ; the Pent it was called. We were deep in the struggles that produced *Romance* and Mr. Conrad was telling me— as he has told me in several kingdoms, shires, duchies, countries and languages—that I did not

know how to write. . . . At any rate we were
engrossed. . . .

A man went past the window : very tall, casting
a shadow across the pink monthly roses. These
commonplace Kentish flowers peeped over the
window sill of the deep, living-room whose low
dappled ceiling was cut in half by a great beam. So
the tall man's shadow flickered across them. . . .

It is disturbing when you, a man of letters,
engrossed in the Heart of the Country, see a shadow
fall from a very tall stranger across your room and
the monthly roses. You think of duns, bailiffs, un-
paid butcher's bills. . . . But Mr. Conrad, always
sanguine, hoping for the best (I never had many hopes
when strangers approached me) exclaimed : "That
will be the man who wants to buy a horse!" Panic
anyhow, seized me : Dans un grenier comme on est
bien a vingt ans! (I suppose I was twenty-four!)
A panic! The immensely tall stranger repassed the
window.

Conrad went to the door. And I heard :

Conrad : You've come about the mare !

Voice : I'm Hudson !

Conrad : She's out with the ladies.

Voice : I'm Hudson !

Conrad : The mare will be back in about half-an-
hour. . . .

Mr. Hudson was staying at New Romney—which
is New only in the sense that William I. built it in
1080 A.D. instead of Cæsar in 45 B.C. . . . Mr.
Hudson then, was staying at New Romney and had
walked over—fourteen miles in order to pay his
respects to the author of *Youth, Heart of Darkness,
Lord Jim,* and *Almayer's Folly.* . . .

I remember Mr. Hudson again—these are more reminiscences !—in one of the cafes in Soho. There were present various writers. And just as one of them—it might have been myself—was shouting " Glorious County, Sussex ! "—in came Mr. Hudson.

The dialogue went on like this :

Writer : Glorious county, Sussex ! Glorious county, Sussex ! You can ride from the Crystal Palace to Beachy Head with only four checks !

Five ! said Mr. Hudson. It was like the crack of doom ; like the deep voice of a raven ; like the sound of a direful bell.

Writer : Only four checks ! There's Wucking, and Cucking ! and Ducking and . . .

" Five ! " said Mr. Hudson.

Writer : Only four checks ! (He used a great many gesticulations, telling the names off on his fingers.) There are Wucking and Cucking and Ducking and Hickley . . .

" Five ! " said Mr. Hudson.

The writer repeated the queer names of Sussex villages. Then Mr. Hudson said :

" East Dean ! " The writer threw his hand violently over his head as one used to see people do on the Western front : then began to tear, immediately afterwards, at his ruffled hair. He exclaimed : " My God ! What a fool I am ! " and stated that he was a Sussex man : bred and born in Sussex : had never been out of Sussex for an instant in his life : had ridden every day from the Crystal Palace to Beachy Head. Yet he had forgotten East Dean.

All the while Mr. Hudson sat motionless, grave, unwinking, gazing at his victim with the hypnotic glare of a beast of prey. Or as if he were studying a new specimen of the genus Fringillago !

III.

And I daresay that is how Mr. Hudson, "gets his effects": gazing at his subject with the expressionless passion of a bird of prey : keeping as still as a tree ; and then cutting down words to nothing. For the three words : the reiterated "Five" and the final "East Dean," convinced one that Mr. Hudson had lived on the South Downs all his life and that you could trust him to take you from Bramber to Findon in pitch black night. Whereas the thousands of words that the other writer poured out only made you doubt that he had ever been in Sussex.

Yet Mr. Hudson was born in the Argentine, of New England stock, and when he came to England he was the first member of his family to set foot on these Islands for 250 years. So maybe he descends from the Navigator. At any rate from those facts which may or may not be facts—we may get certain glimpses of Mr. Hudson's secret. For Mr. Hudson is a secret and mysterious alchemist just as much as, or much more than, Dr. Dee.

Perhaps, owing to his Argentine birth and long racial absence from these Islands, Mr. Hudson has escaped the infection of the amateurish way we handle the language when we write : he has escaped the Authorised Version and the Morte d'Arthur and some one's Rabelais and some one else's Montaigne and Sir Thomas Browne's *Urn Burial*, and all the rest of it. (I may as well put down here what I

meant when I said just now that Stephen Crane said
the most illuminating thing I ever heard as to the
English prose of to-day. He was talking about the
author of *Travels in the Cevennes,* and he said : " By"
God ! when Stevenson wrote : ' With interjected
finger he delayed the action of the time piece,'
meaning ' he put the clock back,' Stevenson put
back the clock of English fiction 150 years." . .
Stevenson, as you know, was the sedulous ape of
Walter Pater or some one like that, and decked
himself out in allusions, borrowed words, stolen
metaphors, inversions and similes for all the world
like Charles Lamb or a Tommy coming back from
the Line hung about with souvenirs.) Well, Mr.
Hudson has escaped all that. You would, as I
have said, think he had never read a book in his
life. Certainly he never read a book and carried off
a phrase like "interjected finger" to treasure it as
Ole Bill might treasure an Iron Cross raped from the
breast of General Humpfenstrumpfen, lately deceased.
Then too, born in the Argentine in remote ages, Mr.
Hudson had the advantage of seeing the light in a
Latin country—at least I suppose nineteenth-century
Argentina *was* a Latin country—and so he was
among a population who used words for the expression
of thoughts. For, among us Occidentals, it is only
the Latin races who use words as clean tools, exactly,
with decency and modesty. You may see the same
in the prose of Mr. Cunninghame Graham who was
also of South American origin. And just as he has
escaped our exhausted use of the language so he has
escaped our conventionally insular way of looking at
a hill, a flower, a bird, an ivy leaf. Yesterday I
picked the first cuckoo flower and the first kingcup

of the year.　When I got my hand well on the stem
of the first I exclaimed :

> "When lady smocks all silver white
> Do tint the meadows with delight . . ."

I daresay I was misquoting, but I felt proud of myself and did not look at the flower.

When I picked the kingcup I said:

> "*Shine like fire in swamps and hollows grey.*" And

I felt proud of myself and did not look at the flower.

When I hear my first skylark I shall spout:

> "Hail to thee, blithe spirit,
> Bird thou never wert . . ."

and for the nightingale it will be: "Most musical;
most melancholy!" . . . and I shan't much look at,
or listen to, either fowl.　And it is the same with all
us English writers.

But, coming from afar, Mr. Hudson looks at all
these things with new eyes and has an air of consummate and unending permanence wherever he may
happen to be, a weather worn air as of an ancient
tree, an ancient rock, a very old peasant.　Wherever
you find him in his writings he will seem to have
been there for ages and to be time-stained to the
colour of the hedgerows, the heather, the downs or the
country people.　So he fits in and the trees, birds, or
shepherds are natural when he is about.　Mr. Hudson
himself is conscious of the fact, for he writes of
Wiltshire in the opening pages of the *Shepherd's
Life:* "Owing to a certain kind of adaptiveness in
me, a sense of being at home wherever the grass
grows, I am in a way a native of Wiltshire too." . . .
And he is a native of Argentina, and La Plata, and
Patagonia and Hampshire and the Sussex downlands
—wherever the grass grows.　That is perhaps the

best gift that has been given to him by the Good
God who has made him such a great poet. For
simple people, shepherds, bird-catchers, girls wheeling
perambulators, old women cleaning front steps,
South American Dictators, gamblers, duellists, birds,
beasts, and reptiles, have been natural before him ;
and the green earth and the sombre trees and the
high downs and the vast Pampas have been just
themselves before him. He looked at them with the
intent gaze of the bird of prey and the abandonment
of the perfect lover.

IV

Twenty-five years ago—really twenty-five years
ago—I lay on my back on the top of the great
shoulder of the downs above Lewes—looking into
the crystalline blue of the sky. There drifted above
me frail, innumerable, translucent, to an immense
height, one shining above the other, like an innumerable company of soap bubbles—the globelike seeds of
dandelions, moving hardly perceptibly at all in the
still sunlight. It was an unforgettable experience.
. . . And yet it wasn't my experience at all. I have
never been on that particular down above Lewes,
though I know the downs very well. And yet I am
not lying ! In the 'nineties of last century, I read
that passage in *Nature in Downland*—and it has
become part of my life. It is as much part of my
life as my first sight of the German lines from a
down behind Albert in 1916 . . . which is about the
most unforgettable of my own experiences in the
flesh. . . . So Mr. Hudson has given me a part of
my life. . . . Indeed, I have a whole Hudson-life

alongside my own . . . and such great pleasure with it. That is what you mean when you say a man is a creator . . . a creative artist. He gives to the world vicarious experience. And such immense pleasure !

And Mr. Hudson does all this with such simple words : there is no child that cannot understand all the words that he uses. That is one of the qualities ; it is the first of the qualities of such masters as are universal in appeal.

VIII

MR. JOSEPH CONRAD AND ANGLO-SAXONDOM

" You will remember, oh Gringoire," so wrote a friend the other day to the Writer, "that it is now some ten or fifteen years since I prophesied that our friend Conrad's *Chance*, then in the veriest embryo, would sell fourteen thousand copies. . . . Why fourteen I hardly know—except for the fact that Great Britain contains fourteen thousand railway stations, so that in talking of a vastly—oh an immensely vastly successful book, in those days we should say that one copy might be found in every village in England, Scotland, and Wales. It is a humble aspiration for one's hero—and to what an extent, in those days, was not Conrad our hero !—a humble aspiration, a thought very humiliating for this England of ours ! The best that, in our wildest dreams we could hope for our Greatest Writer in the World was that one copy of one of his books should penetrate into each village of our country that is possessed of a railway station. And there are thousands and thousands whose names are not recorded in *Bradshaw's Railway Guide*. . . .

" You will remember that occasion, for you have often, since, recurred to it. . . . Well, during the first Battle of the Somme, I received a letter saying that *Chance* had sold its fourteenth thousand copy and reminding me of my prophesy. . . . It occurs to me now to ask you two questions:

" A. Why did I feel that conviction ? For it was a conviction so sure that it seemed as stable as the sunlight on that day, or as the great view bathed in sunlight seen from the place in which, you will remember, our conversation took place.

" B. Why is it that *Chance* did thus set the seal of success on our friend's career that had hitherto been so full of vicissitudes ; that had been so incredibly persevered in ? "

79

Thus, our friend ! . . . His question A. is fairly unanswerable. No one can say for certain why he should have felt his conviction, though feel it he undoubtedly did. Perhaps his subconscious mind argued for him that *Chance* would take ten years to finish; that in ten years the tremendous dynamic force that Mr. Conrad always put into his books must push its way through even the solid wall that, it is said, Anglo-Saxon want of receptivity opposes to any new form in art—to any form of art at all. It is certain that our friend did not feel the same certainty as to the *Rescue* which in those days was in a more advanced state than *Chance* but which struck him as being thinner and more pale—as indeed, to-day it strikes the Writer. It is as if it had been too much written over, too long in the hatching, and in the end not immensely thought out —as if it were indeed a sequel to *Almayer's Folly* from which the enthusiasm had died. . . .

But it is always a difficult problem: Does long acquaintance—immensely long intimacy—with the work of a writer make his later work of necessity seem more pale in the later years; or does the work itself, in any given instance, grow tired ? . . . . No one will ever give the answer to that question. It is very possible that a reader, a young man, coming first to the *Rescue* might find it as overwhelming an experience as, to us who were then young, was the reading of *Almayer's Folly* and *The Nigger of the Narcissus*. And to that supposed reader— How he is to be envied !—these two last might read thin by comparison with the *Rescue*. They—or at least certainly *Almayer*—were written under the strong influence of Daudet, so that they are relatively

limpid and unmannered. . . . At any rate our friend,
the writer of the letter quoted, had no such conviction
as to the *Rescue*—which in the ordinary course
should have appeared well before *Chance*. . . . In
those days Mr. Conrad had groups of followers whose
devotion was final and implicit ; few enough in actual
thousands they were determined to push this great
poet into the illustrious place of his certain inheritance
and each book as it came out added a few more—
until it was merely a matter of a book that should
have a certain popular, but not necessarily vulgar
appeal. . . . That, in effect was the process that our
friend's subconscious mind must have worked out
for him.

To our friend's Question B the answer may
probably be found in the fact that during the whole
of his life Mr. Conrad has made a study of what is
called technique—a study more agitated, more determined and more masterful than can be recorded of
any writer whose name occurs to the mind. Of any
writer ! Remember the despairing letters of Flaubert
to La Muse ; to the authoress of *Consuelo ;* the
eternal and loud dejection, the vociferous anguish,
the enormous Berserker gestures, because Flaubert
could not at times find the real right word—*le mot
juste*—or the exactly satisfying architecture for one or
other of his works. Mr. Conrad suffered more in his
searches—and suffered with a passion more silent . . .

Let us now digress for a moment to consider the
vexed word *technique* that is cried down whenever
two or three English Men of Letters are gathered
together. It was a part of the strategy that in the
'forties and 'sixties of the last century led the Roman-
tics of France and the Pre-Raphaelites of England to

épater les bourgeois ; it is indeed a part of the strategy of all artists who are neither Parnassian nor Academic to retain up the sleeve—whatever else they give away !—some one little mystery of their equipment that shall goad to fury critics or rivals more sluggish of mind.   So it is with this word.

There is no mystery at all about either the object or the practice of technique ; yet the mere use of the word is sufficient to goad many writers into frenzies in which they will strangely betray their real natures ! In itself, the acquiring, the study of, one's particular technique, is nothing more mysterious in its aim or pursuit than the desire of the artist to please—to be interesting ; to be pellucid !   It is nothing more than that.   There is probably no one set of rules that will unite all writers.   There is probably no single rule at all—except that the writer should never bore his reader ! . . .   And even to that rule Richard Wagner proclaimed an exception when he announced the doctrine of Fatigue. . . . He said, in effect, that if you could wear your hearer out sufficiently, at the psychological moment you might introduce a ravishing passage that would be enormously enhanced by the suffering that had gone before. . . . For a writer that is dangerous tactics : a reader may fling a novel into the fire at any moment ; whereas the audience of an opera cannot so easily escape before the composer shall have introduced his ravishing passage. . . . It might perhaps be more just to say that the object of a writer when he sets out to acquire a technique is simply the acquiring of a formula or a habit of mind in which he shall be most pleasing to a large body of his fellow men.   That is a practice that is common to every artist.   The present writer once asked one

of our most enormously popular novelists why,
although he had served in the Army, in one of his
books he represented a major as the superior officer
to a colonel ; and why, in another, the heroine having
married one peer and disliking him, just married
another member of the House of Lords without
waiting to become a widow or to submit to the
tiresome exigencies of the Divorce Courts? The
Novelist's answer was :

" Well. That is what my readers want. They
know that ' major ' means ' larger ' ; and to them a
Divorce Court is a disreputable place so that they
want not to be reminded of its existence. I make it
a rule, for the same reason, never to let my hero or
heroine meet at a dance. At a sale of work or a
charity bazaar : yes ! But never at a dance ! "

This may seem incredible ; yet it is an unexag-
gerated record of the reason given. And, if the
instance may seem to introduce the Reader into the
bas fonds of the pursuit of literature, the illustration is
at least clear enough. . . . Here was a writer as to
whom at least four million inhabitants of Anglo-
Saxon territory would have declared that he was a
Great Writer announcing what was his technique.
He made this a rule ; he made that a rule ! He
found that thus he pleased his readers. Having
pleased them he did not need to trouble about *le mot
juste* ; about architectonics, cadences. . . . The writer
only remembers one sentence from the works of this
novelist. It was this :

" He drank his coffee with cruelly smiling lips that seemed
to gaze into the depths of the cup as if they would pluck its
secret thence ! "

The least number of copies of a single book by this writer purchased by the Anglo-Saxon Publics was six hundred thousand. There are in Great Britain fourteen thousand railway stations.

It may as well be added that the writer once put to this novelist, who was a pleasant, good fellow, the question :

" Why have you, with your prodigious popularity, not ever ventured the final cast of the die with the populace ? Why have you never written a play ? "

Mr. X. answered with serious modesty :

" Well, you see, I have not got the dramatic gift. I am a realist, like Wells and Galsworthy." (Those are the exact two names that he mentioned.) He was pleased to add : " Of course I am not a stylist like you. But a realist. People in my books talk exactly as people do in real life and things only happen as they happen in real life. There is nothing melodramatic about my gift, I am a realist."

The above conversation of a poor fellow now dead is not given in any spirit of mockery. The late novelist was a perfectly honest and conscientious literary phenomenon. He took his work seriously and made an immense fortune by doing his best. He did, that is to say, his best for the Reader that he knew—for the Reader who disliked the idea of the Divorce Courts, of dances, and who considered that a colonel must be junior in rank to a major because the word " major " means " greater."

Opportunities for insight into the unscreened mind of a writer of prodigious popularity must be rare. At any rate they have been rare for the present writer. But indeed opportunities of insight into the mind of any writer are rare enough—into the mind with the

screen off! We wielders of the pen are not only
adepts at misrepresentation of our motives; we are
also adepts at self-deception.   Renan says somewhere
that as soon as one begins to write about oneself one
begins to " poetise "—ever so little, possibly, but still
to poetise ! And this makes the study of literary
methods and the acquiring of a technique the difficult
matters that they are.   You have, if you want to
know how a certain great writer gets his effects, to
go to his works of the imagination, not to his criti-
cisms ; you have, if you want to get at the main-
springs of his cosmic theories, to go, neither to his
autobiography, nor to his letters—but again to his
works of art.   You must study these word by word ;
cadence by cadence and paragraph ; and then, going
back again to the beginning of each paragraph, you
must read it through swiftly so as to get the general
effect . . . And still more, you must ask yourself
over and over again : Why did this writer think out
these words, these vowel colourings, these rhythms,
these cadences ? He thought them out of course, so
that he might please the Reader. But why did he
think that they would please the Reader ? . . . If you
find the answer to this last question you will have
discovered the secret of your author's technique.

Mr. Conrad's researches into the will-to-please-
elevated-into-a-method—into, then, the technique of
various writers have been extraordinarily deep and he
has pursued that study for the whole of his life.
Beginning with Fenimore Cooper, a great stylist,
and Captain Marryat, a great novelist, before he ever
had thought to " saisir la plume," he had come, whilst
still in the forecastle, and whilst merely acquiring the
English language, across, let us say, the Authorised

Version, Mrs. Henry Wood, *The Family Herald*—
the singular tohu-wa-bohu of muddled, half-dis-
integrating books that any one of us must come
across, if, avid of the mere printed page, one travels
much across or around the globe.   He " came across,"
in fact, the very great and the very popular, cheek by
jowl.   And of course, Cooper, Marryat, the English
Bible, *Sartor Resartus*, and the *Ride to Khiva*, and
Mrs. Henry Wood—or it may have been Miss Braddon
that sound constructor of novels and competent
mistress of the Queen's English—these names, then,
are the merest indications of an immense body of
reading, carried on between landfalls and departures,
in docks, or on the high seas. . . .

And preceding, along with, and subsequent to
this omnivorescence of English books, went Mr.
Conrad's intense study of the great French writers.
You may put it that he was able to tell the " difference" between Ponson du Terrail and Gautier or
between the authors of the *Mystères de Paris*
and *La Maison Tellier*.   And undoubtedly the
Author of *Lord Jim* never fell intensely under the
influence of *Lady Audley's Secret*, though to some
small extent he may have fallen under those of
The Two Admirals and *Percival Keene*.   But, except
for Cooper, it is to be doubted if any English
writer had ever much purely literary influence on
this great writer of English.   You have, however,
only to read a passage of description in *The Two
Admirals*—a passage describing a view from cliffs
over a fog at sea, and the topsails of a great fleet
appearing as the fog subsided—to realise how profoundly that great and austere American stylist influenced at least the vision of Mr. Conrad.   Otherwise

we may safely assert that the only influence that
the Englishry have established upon the Author of
Under Western Eyes—that tremendous masterpiece
—have been purely temperamental. Mr. Conrad
has gradually so soaked himself in the English point
of view—and has not the whole globe so soaked
itself?—that he has, in the end, given to Anglo-
Saxondom the most attractive, the most pleasant, the
most desirable of all views of . . . itself. This con-
summation came about with *Chance*. It was
nevertheless fated.

The loom of England through the mists of
Central European politics, the loom of England on
the High Seas, have for so long been so grandiose, or
so perfidious. . . . There are few Polish or Balkan
notables of a certain age to-day who will not tell you,
as a reminiscence of their childhood, of mysterious
night comings and goings, in Ukrainia, in Volhynia,
of whispered conferences. . . . These were said to be
the secret agents of Lord Palmerston, fomenting
combinations and uprisings, offering that *or Anglais*
that the rest of the world has always regarded as
having so profoundly influenced its destinies. And
what seaman can have escaped the profound marks
that the fleets of England have made on the shores
and inlets of the world! . . .

And, perforce, the inhabitants of East-Central
Europe have been for generations enraged politicians.
The present writer happens, by the merest coincidence,
whilst in so apparently unpropitious a place as
Officers' Quarters, to have come across an immense
body of correspondence written by Mr. Conrad to a
compatriot whilst he himself was still at sea. The
letters were voluminous; the sentences impassioned.

. . . If England would only do this against Russia.
. . . If England would only realise. . . . If England
would only join with France in Bulgaria. . . . Always, and always : If England would only . . .

That at least was the main note. And the writer
is indulging in no eavesdropping in making more
significant what is cried out from every page of Mr.
Conrad's romances. . . . That is that, if the literary
influence of France is overwhelming over the style,
the construction of the sentences, the cadence, the
paragraph or the building up of the effects, the profound, the sole, the all-embracing influence on the
point of view is that of this country. . . . And
indeed, if no writer—not even Flaubert—is more
French in his purely literary equipment, none is less
a compatriot of Flaubert in his point of view.

There is a matchless passage in *Lord Jim*—that
in which the battered, obese and unprosperous French
lieutenant, crossing his fat hands across his stomach,
like an Abbé—or like one of the priests in Turgenev's *Fathers and Children*—the dilapidated naval
lieutenant exclaims : " *Ah, mais l'honneur* . . ." . . .
If that is to say, *L'honneur* is gone, life is indeed
finished. And this remark Marlow, the narrator,
blankly " turns down " as inscrutable. For, from the
English point of view, which Mr. Conrad has so
wonderfully given to the world, you may lose your
honneur and may yet retain your honour—and may
yet live. . . . For *l'honneur* is *L'honneur du métier*
for which there is no English translation. You might
say that *l'honneur* is that sense of responsibility to
the fitness of things that, in Anglo-Saxondom is never
enjoined on any soul other than let us say on naval
cadets or infantry privates.

The difference is perhaps most fittingly illustrated by an anecdote of a Conway boy that Mr. Conrad tells somewhere, though the writer has been unable to recapture it. It took place upon a ship in Table Bay, the wind having gone suddenly round and blowing inshore, a hurricane. . . . One of the apprentices on board was a Conway boy; or it may have been a third mate who had been a Conway boy. At any rate it was this boy's job to see that the iron links of the cables were properly stowed away. . . . Mr. Conrad—and indeed the whole of the British mercantile marine—has a peculiar affection for boys who have been trained on the " Conway." They are the well-trained, the fine, the gallant youngsters of a magnificent service. And, in talking of this particular boy Mr. Conrad wrote with a peculiar glow of reminiscence—as one writes of one's days of first love and first hero-worship. . . . Yet this boy had completely neglected to superintend the taking of the anchor on board. So the wind rose—and the anchor would not run out. . . . The boy, then, at the risk of his life, at the expense of extreme agility and "nerve" aided the anchor to run out. Without that the ship would have been lost with all hands.

A French boy in the mercantile marine of France might of course just as well have committed that very horrible crime—and, having committed it might well have failed to display either sufficient agility or sufficient nerve to put the matter right. . . . But he would have felt that he had been *atteint dans l'honneur;* the English boy merely expected and no doubt received what yesterday we used to call a most infernal strafing. . . . And indeed the whole of *Lord Jim* is a parable on that theme. . . . We have the perpetually analytical Marlow pursuing Jim's case round the world. Lord Jim had failed upon just such a point of professional honour : he had been one of several who had taken to their boats leaving a ship crowded with Oriental pilgrims to its fate. . . . The ship did not sink ; was salved and brought into an Eastern port. Lord Jim's dereliction was discovered to the world and he was cashiered, or whatever was the term that is used in the merchant navy. . . .

He was straight, fair, honourable, instinct with the generosities of youth. In his after years he displayed courage, honour, the generosities of true love, heroism ; the splendours of clean youth. . . . And the narrator, Marlow, pursues Lord Jim's "case" round the world. . . .

He pursues it with sympathy, with comprehension infinite, with love, with regret. The French naval lieutenant dismisses it and Jim with the words : "*Ah, mais, l'honneur!*" Lord Jim has sinned against the *esprit du métier*. That finishes him. . . . He may continue, to breathe, to live, to drag out in an underworld an *existence quelconque*. But as a "case" he is nothing. He ceased to exist when he saw sparks before his eyes and considered them to be the sinking masthead lights of the s.s. "Patna."

Mr. Conrad has said that every work of art has a profound moral significance ; and there is scarcely any work of Mr. Conrad's that does not propound some moral enigma, most usually of a political kind. Or perhaps to say "most usually" puts the matter too strongly. Nevertheless the works of Mr. Conrad that the present writer most tremendously remember are *Heart of Darkness, Nostromo, Under Western Eyes*---

that finest novel in the English language—and *The Secret Agent*, that immense failure of comprehension ! Each of these is a political parable, and so, you might add is *An Outpost of Progress;* and so, for the matter of that, is, with its atmosphere of Arab and Malay intrigue beneath the shadow of Dutch suzerainty, Mr. Conrad's first book, *Almayer's Folly*.

Or let us say that each of them is a study, either of humanity beneath an alien yoke, or—as in the case of *Nostromo*—a study of a Utopia. For the Republic of Costaguana, as portrayed in *Nostromo*, is a study, really, of some immense Nowhere. Whatever Costaguana may be it is no Central American Republic ; just as the immense figure of the capataz de cargadores is an immense Everyman, prostrate under the power of Gold—or the Silver of the Mine ! *The Secret Agent*, again, is a study in comparative detectives of another wonderfully projected Nowhere. There are policemen of a Kingdom that is not the United one of Great Britain and Ireland; there is the Agent Provocateur of a Kingdom whose seaboard touches on that of the Kingdom of Bohemia; there is a Great British Politician who is a Sir William Vernon Harcourt enlarged to the scale of elephantiasis and intelligent beyond the dreams of any politician ; and there is a London that may be to be seen in Malaysia, but in few other places.

And this London of *The Secret Agent* lets us into a secret of Mr. Conrad's immense appeal to his fellow men—into the secret of his universality. Other writers would render a London that is just London. Mr. Conrad gives us the Eternal City that floats in the minds of an immense company of men. . . .

" Through the park railings," the foreign police spy was observing London, " his glances beheld men and women riding in the Row, couples cantering past harmoniously, others advancing sedately at a walk. . . . Carriages went bowling by, mostly two horse broughams with here and there a victoria with the skin of some beast inside and a woman's face and hat emerging above the folded hood. And a peculiar London sun—against which nothing could be said except that it looked bloodshot—glorified all this by its stare. It hung at a moderate elevation above Hyde Park Corner with an air of punctual and benign vigilance. The very pavement under Mr. Verloc's feet had an old gold tinge in that diffused light in which neither wall, nor tree, nor beast, nor man cast a shadow. . . ."

That, of course, is not the London of the Londoner who, self-protectively bent upon his personal errand, observes nothing since everything is familiar, ordinary —and indispensable to make up the immense, quiet thing that, to the Londoner, London is. This is not to say that Mr. Conrad's London is not vivid, with its small shops, underground regions, places where suspect articles in yellow envelopes are passed over counters—and with its incredible and for ever memorable four-wheeler !

It is, this place, triumphantly A City—but a city, rather of the human soul than any place in topography. Similarly the Anarchists of *The Secret Agent* are Anarchists of Nowhere : the Enemies of any society, not the disciples of Kropotkin, Bakunin or Reclus with whom we used to be familiar enough. . . . And the police are police evolved from theories of police-men—more psychologically and less venially corrupt than any police of London. You could not imagine Mr. Conrad's Policeman blackmailing brothels and gaming houses : on the other hand, you cannot, easily,

imagine any police as wooden-minded as are Mr.
Conrad's police. . . .

And yet that is really Mr. Conrad's secret—the
secret of his immense appeal. For, whatever he is
or is not, he is not provincial. He is not provincial
to London, to Malaysia, certainly not to Poland—not
even to the sea, or to England. His London is not
the almost ignored placidity that London is to the
Londoner: it is a place observed and rendered, down
to its minutest normalities, with all the keenness that
Flaubert put into his observation of the accordion
cap of Charles Bovary. . . .

That, then, is a technical rule of this great artist
as it was of the immense genius of Croisset. You
might formulate it thus :

"Never take for granted any special knowledge
in your reader!" For your Reader, will be Man,
Woman, New Yorker, inhabitant of Tokio, or seller
of groceries behind a counter in Athens . . . or denizen
of a century that shall come two thousand years after
your own age. If, this rule implies, you have occasion
to take your characters somewhere in a four-wheeler
—let the four-wheeler be projected as the dingy,
rattling, glazed box on shaky wheels that the London
four-wheeler used to be. If you just say: "They
went in a four-wheeler" the lady who will read you
in Vienna or the gentleman in the year A.D. 4920,
will fail to understand you and there will be a white
spot on your page. . . .

That is at any rate one of the secrets of universality.
We may doubt whether Mr. Conrad's Malaysia is in
the least like any districts ruled over by the rajah
lauts ; we may be certain that there is no Republic of
Costaguana ; it may be to us incontrovertible that

Mr. Conrad's London is not the London of the Londoner or Mr. Conrad's sea any known ocean. . . . But the human heart as recorded in Mr. Conrad's pages is the human heart of an immense number of men in all ages and in all climes. . . . So that just as Bunyan's *Pilgrim's Progress* finds innumerable readers in Bohemia and also in the State of Maryland, so Mr. Conrad's books penetrate into the suburbs of London or on Manhattan Beach. . . . And it is a greater feat to be read by commuters and season ticket holders than by half-starved peasantries! For civilisation such as that of ours to-day is an airless thing in which die all the humanities. . . .

To fight out through its rarefied atmosphere either you must know very deeply the deep secrets of the human heart—or you must know and avail yourself of the fugitive pettinesses of the pettiest folk of your day. The popular novelist who knew that millions and millions of human beings in England and America regarded a dance as a sinful place for the meetings of the immaculate, and knew also that these millions crave to read of immaculate central characters, had a knowledge of certain human weaknesses. . . . But these weaknesses soon cease to be millionwise characteristics—then the popular novel dies. Probably it fulfils a function : there is no doubt latent in all humanity the necessity to have the mind lightly massaged by infinitesimal sensations and few, even of the greatest thinkers can do without the stream of contemptible imbecilities that are to be found in the daily press. We need, in fact, gossip to fill up voids in the chinks of thought and it does not much matter how fugitive may be the interest or how untrue to even imaginable fact the gossip may be. . . . Only : the greatest of scandals loses its attractiveness in nine days; within the day the page of the daily paper becomes as repulsive as cold cooked flat-fish; the page of the popular novel is dead the minute after it is turned.

But a great talent occupies itself with the deep places of the mind and frames its projections of those secrets in projections of kingdoms that are the kingdoms not merely of to-day. . . . So it is with Mr. Conrad.

The reader may well say that there is here a contradiction. The writer has said that Mr. Conrad is the most English of the English; the most un-French of the un-French; and yet the writer now alleges that Mr. Conrad is in no way provincial. . . . Surely to be the most English of the English is to be the most provincial of provincials ! . . . But that is not the case. . . .

Englishism is a frame of mind extraordinarily universal, in strata, throughout the world—the frame of mind of all men who are extraordinarily amateurish in all matters psychological, moral or pertaining to the sentiments. And, as a counterpoise such men are singularly practical—or at least desire to be extraordinarily practical in all material aspects. . . . So you have Mr. Conrad's Marlow, extremely capable of taking care of himself, possessed, as are few master mariners of " means "; so that, when he will, he can leave the sea and dwell here or there— pursuing all the world over unsolvable moral problems that to almost any French Frenchman can be dismissed with four words : " *Ah, mais l'honneur !* "

But there are men of all races, of all ages, who have dismissed, formularised and settled their material

needs. They have their farms, their *rentes*, their
valets, their automobiles, their brands of soap, their
knowledges of how to handle venial police or to
swim through the meshes of laws against profiteering.
These men have, however, never faced any moral
problems at all subtle, so that when a really subtle
moral or ethical point is forced irresistibly up against
their attentions, they are extraordinarily at sea. The
problem will loom up, large beyond any reasonable
proportion ; they will seek for its solution, talking to
person after person, half across the world, half through
life. . . . These are the English of the world, whether
they be born in Kent, in Dublin, in Berlin or in New
York, on Ninth Avenue between 23rd and 29th
Streets. . . . They are the peoples of settled material
circumstances who have lost so much time over those
settlings that they have never looked at moral
problems. So moral problems have for them an
extraordinary attraction. . . .

Mr. Conrad reveals himself as little in his books
as does Shakespeare in his plays. Nevertheless no
author, however rigid his technique of self-conceal-
ment, can conceal utterly his moral or material pre-
ferences—at least in his characters. And it is perfectly
discernible what type of man Mr. Conrad, let us say,
would prefer to live with. That is the great crite-
rion. . . . And Mr. Conrad chooses for his companions
—the Writer is in no sense referring to any other
than those most intimate companions of an author,
his Characters—men slightly obtuse, men extremely
well able to look after their investments, their to-
morrow's food, their purchases of real estate or of
commercial vessels. Even his seamen are practically
never the Jack ashore of the popular view—not

Captain Whalley, not Falk, not the Rajah Laut of *Almayer's Folly* and of *The Rescue*, not any of the dour First or Second mates. . . . The nearest he comes to the *tapageur* spirit of life is in Kurtz of *Heart of Darkness*, the Belgian Jack ashore who, set free from the rules of painting, ornaments his Congo stockade with the skulls of captives eaten by his cannibal troops. Excess of any kind is singularly lacking in this author's pages. So that the embrace in *A Smile of Fortune* strikes Mr. Conrad's diligent reader, mild though it be, as, by contrast almost pornography.

It is not of course anything of the sort: it is an artistic effort to gauge the relative values of transient passion and of potatoes, in the Anglo-Saxon world. Passion is not of course absent from this author's works but, when present it is reduced to its proper secondary place in the Anglo-Saxon scale of things. Or it is accompanied with the intense searchings of the heart with which the Anglo-Saxon—and possibly also the Slav—renders his passions more poignant, when he indulges in any. Of the passion that is rendered, for instance in *Fort Comme la Mort* of Maupassant, there is not a mention, not a suspicion in all the great range of Mr. Conrad's works—and one imagines Mr. Conrad disapproving of that really greatest of all renderings of atrocious love—of atrociously painful love! He and his compagnons de voyage have other things to do than to wreck their careers on impossible miseries. They have their cargoes—cargoes often sufficiently romantic—to bring into port. . . . And it is characteristic that Mr. Conrad translates the French phrase *Une Bonne Fortune* by the words A SMILE

OF FORTUNE; and that the comment of the Second
Mate, in this case, is "A wonderful piece of
luck!" . . . But those words apply to the price at
which the hero sells his potatoes, not to the uncon-
summated embrace. . . .

It has been said somewhere—and Mr. Conrad has
somewhere corroborated the statement if we do not
mistake—that Mr. Conrad cannot draw a woman.
But that is not true. . . . If we said that Mr.
Conrad's world is a man made world we should be
more near the truth.

For the women in Mr. Conrad's books are omni-
present and various. From the wonderful, wordless
girl in *Falk*, the best constructed of all Mr. Conrad's
short stories, to the English Lady of that comparative
failure *The Rescue*, there is no woman that is not
well-done. Even the almost endless Mrs. Gould of
Nostromo is marvellous. It is only that, in their
functions they are extremely unimportant to the
story. They are the chattels of the hearth, the
occupants of deck-cabins; they hold torches or they
soothe. It is not that Mr. Conrad is afraid of
spoiling his market by dwelling on the relations of
the sexes—as was the case with that miserable
fellow Robert Louis Stevenson. It is simply that
relations of the sexes do not come into his working
life—and by life the writer means, of course, not the
life that Mr. Conrad has lived, but the life that he
has given us.*

To descend for the fifth of a moment to reminiscences, the writer well remembers a speech that Mr.

---

* " Girl! What? Did I mention a girl? Oh she is out of it—
completely. They—the women—I mean—are out of it—should be out of
it. We must help them to stay in that beautiful world of their own, lest
ours get worse." *Heart of Darkness*, volume *Youth*, p. 131, 1902 ed.

Conrad inserted into a collaborated work. . . . It was to the effect that there are men who will derogate from the most sacred duties of friendship :

" For a little money or some woman ! " and the disdain expressed in the last three words was overwhelming. In Mr. Conrad's world, in fact, woman is just "some woman." And it is significant that, in the greatest, wisest and most poetic of all Mr. Conrad's works *Under Western Eyes* there is a rendering of the passion of love crossed by the most final of all ethical scruples, the giving to death of a woman's brother, that is unsurpassed for hopeless yearning by anything except possibly the rendering of the passion for Lavretsky of Lisa in Turgenev's *House of Gentlefolk.* . . . There is in each work the same rendering of pain rendered hopeless, of desire intense but self-frustrated on account of ethical scruples, of self-immolation, of eternal regret. . . . But whereas, in the work of the " beautiful genius " of Russia, the passion is the thing that wrecks the lives of both Lisa and Lavretsky, in the work of our very great poet the lives are wrecked by the concrete material surroundings. . . .

Heaven forbid that the writer should be taken to mean that Mr. Conrad is not quite cynical, or is unaware of the bearings of his works. He has selected his companions—the Englishry—after he has gained an immense knowledge of the lives lived by all the inhabitants of the globe; if we may thus translate the phrase " *il a roulé sa bosse un peu partout !* " . . . He has met innumerable men ; he has read innumerable books ; we may say that no living writer has read more books in the pursuit of that *technique* which consists in the finding out of what it is that appeals to great bodies of men.   And, after these immense readings and these extended Odysseys, Mr. Conrad has elected to select these Islands for his residence, his analyses—and his applause.   It is for these Islands a great honour.   In the days before the War there were three writers whose next productions thinking men awaited with desire.   They were Henry James, Anatole France, and Joseph Conrad. No one else even began to count.   One had one's life, one's merchandisings, one's career, one's guilt. . . . But all these things one would suspend in order to read the latest, or the newest, words of this American, this Frenchman . . . and this Elizabethan.

For to the present writer it has always seemed that Mr. Conrad is an Elizabethan, finding a place somewhere between Shakespeare, the only Elizabethan to be consummate, and the author of the *Duchess of Malfi*.   There is about Mr. Conrad's mind a touch of Ford, of Webster, of Heywood, even of Marlow—his is the same value of life, the same, a little blurred poetic vision.   It was a whole plot, a whole region, that waited for the rendering of a master, since Ford, Kyd, Webster and the rest had only botched at that estate with harrowing, prentice hands.   Mr. Conrad has given it rhythms, organ tones, immense and mournful cadences, dark splendours. . . .

In the end Mr. Joseph Conrad Kurzeniowski is a Pole.   The vile pressure of the Russians drove him from his birthland ; the tides of the sea washed him on to these shores. . . . And it was in Elizabeth's days that Poland was last great.   Or let us put it that Poland had been in a state of suspended animation since the seventeenth century and that English Literature has been insular indeed since the last word of the *Tempest* was written. Mr. Conrad, coming from Poland—even as Henry James coming from New England—has once more put Anglo-Saxondom into contact with the main stream of human art. He has rendered a whole region of the Anglo-Saxon mind that has remained unexplored by any one capable of European appreciation since the days of Elizabeth—that side of the Anglo-Saxon mind that is glamourous, mournful because of its unavailingness in face of the Infinite. . . .

> " . . . What is't to die?
> 'Tis less than to be born. a lasting sleep,
> A quiet resting from all jealousy.
> A thing we all pursue. I do know besides
> It is but giving over of a game
> That must be lost. . . ."

The men of the life that Mr. Conrad thus champions—his compagnons de voyage—are intent always on adventure on the High Seas; they are intent always on maintaining a certain standard of rectitude that yet consorts with a certain " slimness " to make them in the end be always " top-dogs "; they are intent also always on such *bonnes fortunes* as shall not interfere with the selling price of their cargo—of potatoes! . . . They are intent always, that is to say, at once on ethics and their material establishments . . . and Mr. Conrad, who might have rendered, all the world over, all the finenesses of the world, has chosen to render them. . . .

That is a " wonderful piece of good luck," a true smile of fortune—for Anglo-Saxondom!

IX

IN, I think, the year before the War, I published a
monograph on the works of Henry James, and this
work was received by the Press with a violence of
disapproval that can seldom have been equalled. I
have frequently asked myself why this was? Until
that date I had been usually treated by reviewers to
praise that you might have called fulsome – and that
for writing that was exactly similar in tone to that
of the James book; analytical stuff that was not
particularly good but that, rather vaguely and without great purpose or vigour, now and then illuminated
some half-truth or other. What then accounted
for this outcry in a Press usually—let us say—
subservient enough?

I can only imagine, since the crime then generally
laid at my door was want of reverence for the Master!
—that I was suddenly hated because I hatefully
pointed out that this great man was an American.
I do not mean to say that this was an outburst
patriotic in its origins. The Eastern side of the
Atlantic has accepted so many Americans, from
Emerson, to Whistler, and has accepted them so
tacitly that we may be absolved of that sort of
jealousy. . . . No, it was rather as if, all his life, Mr.
James had been trying to conceal a physical blemish

and as if I, flagitiously and like a son of Noah, jeering at an impotence, had torn aside a veil. And this outcry was made by gentlemen who, very obviously, had neither a tenth of my knowledge of the Master's works, nor one hundredth part of my love for the man.

For I do not believe that any human being surpassed or surpasses me in either attribute. And yet, at this moment, I insist on his Americanism. I insist on it because of the very fact that he was in externals so Europeanised. For his Cosmopolitan surface was itself a product of a New England yearning towards a gentler and more glamourous Eastern Continent. That distinctively New England passion this great Master himself rendered in such stories as *The Four Meetings : A Passionate Pilgrim*, or *Europe*. These are tales of simple New England souls who desire to find a Europe of their Transatlantic dreams. And, either physically or figuratively these dreams are frustrated : either they never get to Europe or, getting there, they find, on the rich turf, under the shadows of the great elms and of the ancient spires a human society more mannered but in no shade more spiritualised than is to be found in Colorado. And that was the real tragedy of the Master's life—that he penetrated the Arcana of European mysteries to find only the universal human heart with its greeds, its materialisms and, in the end, its Armageddon of passionate disillusionment. . . .

And indeed, in ascribing to James his full share of Americanism I had had no idea of sneering at him. As far as I am concerned, the United States, I am ready to aver, has played a far larger part in the

development of that European literary tendency that
I have called the Mainstream than ever we have;
and we must give to New England—and indeed to
the United States as a whole—its due of being, in
the Arts, a great deal closer to the mainland of
Europe than is the Mother Country.   Indeed,
between America, France, and Russia, in the nine-
teenth century and in what has passed of the
twentieth there has been a play and interplay of
influences that oddly resembles the constant crossing
and recrossing of currents between France and
Great Britain in the late seventeenth and eighteenth
centuries.   Just as it is extremely difficult to dis-
entangle the influences of Defoe, Rapin, Addison,
Crébillon, Richardson, Marivaux in the earlier epoch,
so it is difficult exactly to estimate the reactions of
Edgar Poe, Baudelaire, James, Maupassant, Turgenev
and so on, right up to the days of Mr. Pound, H.D.,
Mr. Carlos Williams, Mr. T. S. Eliot.   And, if the
only American influence on France of which we can
be certain was that of Poe, that influence was so
great and has proved so lasting that it may well be
said to fairly balance the others.   And indeed, of the
Moderns, Poe may be said to be the only Anglo-
Saxon figure that has any importance at all as a
constructive critic of the technical side of literature,
at any rate during the last century.   And, as I have
frequently pointed out, the Boston-New York of
James and W. D. Howells, that succeeded the pure
Boston of Emerson and Holmes was, even in the
'eighties of last century, a city infinitely more interested
in—more intrigued about—the " how " of Literature
than any to be found in the Islands East of the
Atlantic.   For one thing the great Vested Interest

of militant amateurism never arose in the United
States; for another, the more practical American
mind saw, from the very moment that the great
Turgenev-Flaubert group existed in this world—at
the very rising of that moon—that an apprenticeship
is as necessary in the Arts of Writing as in those of
painting and music and in all of the crafts.

So—I think Mr. Moore so put it—Henry James
came to Europe and studied Turgenev, and Mr.
Howells remained in New York and studied Henry
James. And, in the course of time, unlike Mr.
Conrad, who, born to impracticable Poland, came
to luxuriate in our commercial airs, Henry James,
born to a materialist Puritanism, sought here a
gentler civilisation that he never found. I am aware
that industrious politicians and critics are at this
moment seeking to foment wars between the two
sides of that Atlantic and that others, still more
industriously, are seeking to foment wars between
ourselves and France. So that if I now write
generously of the Arts of either of those Other
Houses I run a great risk of being hung, in a year or
so, as a French or a Yankee spy. But if those
abominations are brought about one may as well be
hung as live. For, in truth, these three nations of
the Atlantic sea-board form one civilisation—a civilisation not of material interests, but of the humanities.
. . . However, it will be fifty years before any Reader
will be found to listen to that sort of Pacifism!

Anyhow, it was much more than W. D. Howells
that remained behind and studied, consciously or unconsciously, Mr. James. It was the whole American
writing craft. There are innumerable witnesses to
this. You have, to-day, say Mrs. Wharton; or you

have the immense output of American magazines
every one of which will contain, month after month,
short stories that are at least well-machined and
smartly narrated. For the matter of that you have
one or two magazines of what is called the "crank"
variety which print really good literature. But the
most striking instance that I ever came across was
Stephen Crane.

It was perhaps in 1896—I am never very certain
of my dates, but it was about then—that Mr. Garnett
brought poor, dear, "Stevie" to call upon me. I
was then living a very self-consciously Simple Life at
Limpsfield in a newly built cottage of huge lumps
of rough stone. These Crane, fresh from the other
side of the world, muddledly took to be the remains
of an ancient fortification. He put in, I remember,
a rose tree beside the immensely thick, oaken front
door—for all the world like a king planting a
memorial oak!—and looking at an outside fire-place
remarked :

"That's a bully ol' battlement!"

He told me afterwards that, although he did not,
in the ordinary way set much store by corner lots and
battle-fields I and my establishment had pretty well
seen him for the jack-pot. But the literary point
about the interview was this :

At a given moment Mr. Garnett said that Crane—
he was then the all-famous author of the *Red Badge
of Courage*—must have read a great deal of French
imaginative literature. Crane said defiantly that he
had never read a word of French in his life. (I
dare say the defiance was to my address far more than
to Mr. Garnett's.) He had been dragged up in the
Bowery, he had, and he hadn't any use for corner lots.

When Mr. Garnett persisted and pointed out the great resemblance of his handling of a story to Maupassant's, Crane said :

"Oh well, I've read ol' man James's . . . " I forget what it was he confessed to having read, but it was one of James's French critical works.

Later, I was requested—this will seem an improbable story—to go one evening to Crane's house at Oxted, near by, to give Mrs. Crane a lesson in dressmaking. The request had been made by a local lady who liked to " bring people together," I not having, out of shyness, I dare say, pursued the acquaintance with Crane. I found Mrs. Crane alone and she did not want a lesson in dressmaking—of the mediæval variety. But she begged me to await Crane's return : he had gone up to town on business and she expected he would be nervous and glad of distraction. I think this was the only unsolicited call I ever paid—and that was due to a misapprehension !—and I was nervous enough myself !

He came back—nervous and distracted, truly, and very late—but extraordinarily glad. I have never again seen such gladness as was displayed on that Oxted-night by that great and elf-like writer. For me, Crane came nearer to the otherworldly being than any human soul I have ever encountered : he was indeed what Trelawny has made us believe Shelley was—the Author of emotionalised fiction.

He kept it exaggeratedly beneath the surface. Superficially he was harsh and defiant enough : his small, tense figure and his normal vocabulary were those of the Man of Action of dime drama—very handy in a Far Western fashion, with a revolver. He loved, indeed, to sit about in breeches, leggings, and

shirt-sleeves, with a huge Colt strapped to his belt.
And he would demonstrate with quite sufficient skill
how, on a hot day he could swat a fly on the wall
with the bead foresight of his " gun "—all the while
uttering Bowery variations on his theme of giving no
fancy prices for antiquities.   He meant by that that
he was not a Poet.

But he was !   I will venture to say that no more
poetic vision of humanity in our late Armageddon
was ever written than the *Red Badge of Courage*
—and that was written twenty years before Armageddon was upon us.   I re-read it—one paid one's
minor re-visitations even then—along with Conrad's
Typhoon, France's *Histoire Comique* and *What
Maisie Knew*, in Bécourt Wood during the first
battle of the Somme.   And, for the life of me, I can
hardly tell which is to me the more real—the dawn
appearing over a host just standing to in Crane's book,
or the dawns that we used to see, between the dusty
thistle stalks, glimmering over those hammered,
violently chiselled and blasted downs.   That was the
sheer instinct of the Poet who searches the hearts of
man—that writing.

What an admirable talent !   You had *Maggie ;*
you had the *Open Boat*, the *Bride Comes to
Yellow Sky*, the *Three White Mice*.   And I remember with particular emotion the *Third Violet*,
a book which Crane's chief admirers did not care for
and one which I have not been able to re-read, since
it appears to be out of print and I have been able to
find no copy.

It is astonishing that any book of Stephen Crane's
should be out of print and that one should be able to
find no copy.   It is lamentable !

He was glad, that night at Oxted ; he was astonishingly glad, the joy shining out of him as heat glows
sometimes through opaque substances—because his
agent, Mr. Pinker, had given him a contract to sign
which guaranteed him £20 per thousand words for
everything that he chose to write and had advanced
him a sum of money sufficient to pay his Oxted debts.
So he could get away from Oxted.   The motive may
seem materialistic to the official-poetic amongst
readers.   But Crane had hated his suburban villa
with a hatred comprehensible enough—and he hated
debts with the hatred of a high-strung, nervous but
realistic poet.

With the falling from his shoulders of that intolerable load he desired, as Mrs. Crane had foreseen,
to talk.   And he talked.   He kept me there listening,
right through the night, until breakfast time.   He
had the most amazing eyes ; large, like a horse's ;
frowning usually with the gaze of one looking very
intently—but shining astonishingly at times.   And a
deep voice.   When he became excited—as that night
he was—the studied Americanisms disappeared from
his vocabulary, or nearly so, and he talked a rathei
classical English.   He planned then, his glorious
future.

They were, his plans, not so much a matter of the
world over which he intended to travel, flinging coins
from the purse of Fortunatus that had been put by
Mr. Pinker into his hands : it was a question, rather,
of how he would render that world when he had
roved all over it.   He talked, in fact, about his
technique.

I do not flatter myself that it was to me that he
talked ; that night he would have talked like that to

a broomstick. . . . I had, I suppose, in those days a Pre-Raphaelite or Æsthetic aspect and he seemed to make me responsible for the poems of Rossetti and the prose of Mr. Legallienne. So that, beginning by telling me, like Mr. Conrad, that I could not write and never should be able to write, he went on to tell me how writing should be done—and from time to time denouncing me.

And his formulæ were those of the Flaubert-Maupassant-Turgenev school. He had read, naturally, a great deal more French than he had chosen to acknowledge in my unsympathetic presence, to Mr. Garnett. I do not mean to say that his native talent and inspiration did not make him a peculiarly good subject for that contagion. He would no doubt have written simply and forcibly and in the most economical of forms if Maupassant had never written a line. But, under that stimulus he had arrived much more quickly at a " method " and he knew quite well " what he was doing."

And what particularly interested me was his projection before me, then, of a great series of heroic poems that he was planning to write—in Vers Libre. Of these he wrote only one volume—the *Black Riders*, and, if, in this verse he did not attain to the quietness and colloquialism, at which he aimed theoretically—and to which I fancy that even at that date I had attained—he certainly showed some of the way for a whole school. He hated both rhyme and formal metre and at one point he shouted at me—he had never seen a word of mine :

" You ruin . . . ruin . . . ruin . . . all your work by the extra words you drag in to fill up metres and by the digressions you make to get at rhymes ! "

He possessed, in fact, in a remarkable degree not only
the Literary Gift but the Literary Sense—and a
devouring passion for words.

The contacts of Henry James and poor Stevie
were peculiar. I do not remember to have heard the
two of them discuss together anything of material
interest.   Indeed I only remember to have seen them
together at large social functions like the flower
shows that Crane and his family interested themselves
in, at Brede in Sussex.   But I heard the two men
discuss each other, often enough.

Crane's attitude towards the Master—except for
occasional lapses of irritation in which he would talk
of James as Henrietta Maria—was boyishly respectful
and enthusiastic. I dare say that, with his marvellous
insight, he valued the great man very sufficiently, and
when his defiant mood was off him and he was not
riding about the country on one of his immense
coach-horses, he would readily enough acknowledge
himself to be, if not a disciple, at least an attentive
scholar of the Old Man's works.

By that time he had taken Brede Place—an
immense, haunted and unrestored Elizabethan manor
house, lying, unhealthily beshadowed and low in a
Sussex valley. I fancy I was responsible for intro-
ducing him to the Place; at any rate I had known it
for many years before he came there. And, with
characteristic enthusiasm, though he would still declare
that he had no use for battle-fields—he led there the
life of an Elizabethan baron. Rushes covered the
floors ; dogs lay beneath the table to gnaw the bones
that fell ; a baron of beef and a barrel of ale stood
always ready near the back door for every tramp to
consume. The house was filled with stray dogs, lost

cats, and, as if in tides, indiscriminately chosen bands
of irresponsible guests, would fill and recede from, the
half-furnished rooms. . . . And in a small room over
the great porch of the house Crane would sit writing,
to keep it all going.

It used to be terrible to see the words, in a tiny
writing, slowly filling the immense sheet of white
foolscap; falling from the pen that made that
passionate pilgrimage, to keep going that immense
house, that not so much riotous as uncalculated
hospitality. It was the brave attempt of a gallant
soul—and surely there was never soul more gallant
than that of Stephen Crane. . . . But the end was
tragic, as it must be in that haunted and foredooming
hollow into which the very sunlight seemed to fall
with the air of a blight.

The Old Man—one called him that as if he had
been the colonel of a regiment or the captain of a
battleship—took his young compatriot very hardly—
almost shudderingly, you might say. Brede was just
within calling distance in a vehicle from Rye, and
James certainly called on Crane often enough to show
a decent cordiality to a young fellow-countryman in
the neighbourhood. I had a great affection—as I
hope I have made plain—for the younger man and,
though I never " presumed " to remonstrate with the
Master when he used to groan over the necessity of
going to Brede, I suppose I made this affection appear
now and then in the tones of my voice. So that once
he said :

"Figure to yourself, my dear H. . . ., what
would be *your* feelings if being, as I hope I may
phrase it, an honoured guest in Baltimore, or one of
our friend Wister's gentler Southern cities, you

should find installed in a place of honour, but laughed at as a peculiar national representative of your own, some—gifted, I grant you : oh surely gifted—but, wholly atrocious for accent and mannerisms. . . . Cockney from the Mile End Road!" That was pretty exactly the beginning of his speech. And he went on to make it plain that what most appalled him was Crane's life of the moment: his aping, so that he seemed to reduce to absurdity, the semi-feudal state of a Tudor lord—on the poor " £20 per thousand." It was as if the Old Man shuddered at seeing a mock made of a settled and august mode of European life ; and shuddered all the more because that very mockery was the sincere expression of admiration by a compatriot. In much the same way he spoke with bitter hatred of Mark Twain's *Yankee at the Court of King Arthur.*

I think I will, after reflection, lay claim to a very considerable degree of intimacy with Henry James. It was a winter, and a wholly non-literary intimacy. That is to say, during the summers we saw little of each other. He had his friends and I mine. He was too often expecting " my friend Lady Maude," or some orthodox critic to tea and I, modern poets whom he could not abide. Occasionally, even during the summer, he would send from Rye to Winchelsea, a distance of two miles, telegrams such as the following which I transcribe :—

" To FORD MADOX HUEFFER, Esq.,

" The Bungalow, Winchelsea, near Rye, Sussex.

" May I bring four American ladies, of whom one a priest, to tea to-day ?

" Yours sincerely, HENRY JAMES."

And he would come.

But, in the winters, when London visitors were
scarce, he would come to tea every other day with
almost exact regularity, and I would walk back with
him to Rye. On the alternate days I would have
tea with him and he would walk back to Winchelsea,
in all weathers, across the wind-swept marshes. That
was his daily, four miles, constitutional.

But it was, as I have said, an almost purely non-
literary intimacy. I could, I think, put down on one
page all that he ever said to me of books—and,
although I used, out of respect, to send him an
occasional book of my own on publication, and he an
occasional book of his to me, he never said a word to
me about my writings and I do not remember ever
having done more than thank him in letters for his
volume of the moment. I remember his saying of
Romance that it was an immense English Plum
Cake which he kept at his bedside for a fortnight and
of which he ate a nightly slice.

He would, if he never talked of books, frequently
talk of the personalities of their writers—not infrequently in terms of shuddering at their social
excesses, much as he shuddered at contact with
Crane. He expressed intense dislike for Flaubert
who "opened his own door in his dressing-gown"
and he related, not infrequently, unrepeatable stories
of the menages of Maupassant—but he much preferred Maupassant to "poor dear old Flaubert." Of
Turgenev's appearance, personality and habits he
would talk with great tendernesses of expression—
he called him nearly always "the beautiful Russian
genius," and would tell stories of Turgenev's charming
attentions to his peasant mistresses. He liked, in

fact, persons who were suave when you met them—
and I daresay that his preference, of that sort
coloured his literary tastes. He preferred Maupassant
to Flaubert because Maupassant was *homme du monde*
—or at any rate had *femmes du monde* for his
mistresses ; and he preferred Turgenev to either
because Turgenev was a quiet aristocrat and invalid
of the German Bathing Towns, to the finger tips.
And he liked—he used to say so—people who
treated him with deep respect.

Flaubert he hated with a lasting, deep rancour.
Flaubert had once abused him unmercifully—over a
point in the style of Prosper Merimée, of all people in
the world. You may read about it in the *Correspondence* of Flaubert, and James himself referred to the
occasion several times. It seemed to make it all the
worse that, just before the outbreak, Flaubert should
have opened the front door of his flat to Turgenev
and James, in his dressing-gown.

Myself, I suppose he must have liked, because I
treated him with deep respect, had a low voice—
appeared, in short, *a jeune homme modeste*. Occasionally he would burst out at me with furious irritation
—as if I had been a stupid nephew. This would be
particularly the case if I ventured to have any opinions
about the United States—which, at that date, I had
visited much more lately than he had. I remember
one occasion very vividly—the place, beside one of
the patches of thorn on the Rye road, and his aspect,
the brown face with the dark eyes rolling in the
whites, the compact, strong figure, the stick raised
so as to be dug violently into the road. He had been
talking two days before of the provincialism of
Washington in the 'sixties. He said that when one

descended the steps of the Capitol in those days *on trébuchait sur des vaches*—one stumbled over cows, as if on a village green. Two days later, I don't know why—I happened to return to the subject of the provincialism of Washington in the 'sixties. He stopped as if I had hit him and, with the coldly infuriated tone of a country squire whose patriotism has been outraged, exclaimed :

" Don't talk such *damnable* nonsense ! " He really shouted these words with a male fury. And when, slightly outraged myself I returned to the charge with his own *on trébuchait sur des vaches*, he exclaimed : " I should not have thought you would have wanted to display such ignorance," and hurried off along the road.

I do not suppose that this was as unreasonable a manifestation of patriotism as it appears. No doubt he imagined me incapable of distinguishing between material and cultural poverties and I am fairly sure that, at the bottom of his mind lay the idea that in Washington of the 'sixties there had been some singularly good cosmopolitan and diplomatic conversation and society, whatever the cows might have done outside the Capitol. Indeed I know that, towards the end of his life, he came to think that the society of early, self-conscious New England, with its circumscribed horizon and want of exterior decoration or furnishings, was a spiritually finer thing than the mannered Europeanism that had so taken him to its bosom. As these years went on, more and more, with a sort of trepidation, he hovered round the idea of a return to the American Scene. When I first knew him you could have imagined no oak more firmly planted in European soil. But, little by little, when he talked

about America there would come into his tones a
slight tremulousness that grew with the months. I
remember, once he went to see some friends—Mrs.
and Miss Lafarge, I think—off to New York from
Tilbury Dock. He came back singularly excited,
bringing out a great many unusually uncompleted
sentences. He had gone over the liner : " And
once aboard the lugger . . . And if . . . Say a tooth-
brush . . . And circular notes . . . And something
for the night . . . And if . . . By Jove, I might
have . . ." All this with a sort of diffident shame-
facedness.

I fancy that his mannerisms—his involutions,
whether in speech or in writing, were due to a settled
conviction that, neither in his public nor in his
acquaintance, would he ever find any one who would
not need talking down to. The desire of the Artist,
of the creative writer, is that his words and his
" scenes " shall suggest—of course with precision—
far more than they actually express or project. But,
having found that his limpidities, from *Daisy Miller*
to the *Real Thing*, not only suggested less than he
desired, but carried suggestions entirely unmeant,
he gave up the attempt at Impressionism of that type
—as if his audiences had tired him out. So he talked
down to us, explaining and explaining, the ramifica-
tions of his mind. He was aiming at explicitness, never
at obscurities—as if he were talking to children.

At any rate, then, he had none of that provincialism of the literary mind which must for ever be
dragging in allusions to some book or local custom.
If he found it necessary to allude to one or the other
he explained them and their provenance. In that
you saw that he had learned in the same school as

Mr. Conrad and as Stephen Crane. And indeed he had.

It has always seemed to me inscrutable that he should have been so frequently damned for his depicting only one phase of life; as if it were his fault that he was not also Mr. Conrad, to write of the sea, or Crane, to project the life of the New York slums. The Old Man knew consummately one form of life; to that he restricted himself. I have heard him talk with extreme exactness and insight of the life of the poor—at any rate of the agricultural poor, for I do not remember ever to have heard him discuss industrialism. But he knew that he did not know enough to treat of farm-labourers in his writing. So that, mostly, when he discoursed of these matters he put his observations in the form of questions : " Didn't I agree to this ? " " Hadn't I found that ? "

But indeed, although I have lived amongst agricultural labourers a good deal at one time or another, I would cheerfully acknowledge that his knowledge—at any rate of their psychologies—had a great deal more insight than my own. He had such an extraordinary gift for observing minutiæ —and a gift still more extraordinary for making people talk. I have heard the secretary of a golf-club, a dour silent man who never addressed five words to myself though I was one of his members, talk for twenty minutes to the Master about a new bunker that he was thinking of making at the fourteenth hole. And James had never touched a niblick in his life. It was the same with market-women, tram-conductors, ship-builders' labourers, auctioneers. I have stood by and heard them talk to him for hours. Indeed, I am fairly certain that he

once had a murder confessed to him. But he needed
to stand on extraordinarily firm ground before he
would think that he knew a world. And what he
knew he rendered, along with its amenities, its gentle-
folkishness, its pettinesses, its hypocrisies, its make-
believes. He gives you an immense—and an
increasingly tragic—picture of a Leisured Society
that is fairly unavailing, materialist, emasculated—
and doomed. No one was more aware of all that
than he.

Stevie used to rail at English Literature, with its
Stevenson and the interjected finger, as being one
immense, petty, Parlour Game. Our books he used
to say were written by men who never wanted to go
out of drawing-rooms for people who wanted to live
at perpetual tea-parties. Even our adventure stories,
colonial fictions and tales of the boundless prairie
were conducted in that spirit. The criticism was just
enough. It was possible that James never wanted to
live outside tea-parties—but the tea-parties that he
wanted were debating circles of a splendid aloofness, of
an immense human sympathy, and of a beauty that
you do not find in Putney—or in Passy!

It was his tragedy that no such five-o'clock ever
sounded for him on the timepieces of this world. And
that is no doubt the real tragedy of all of us—of all
societies—that we never find in our Spanish Castle
our ideal friends living in an assured and permanent
republic. Crane's Utopia, but not his literary method,
was different. He gave you the pattern in—and the
reverse of—the carpet in physical life—in Wars, in
slums, in Western saloons, in a world where the
"gun" was the final argument. The life that Mr.
Conrad gives you is somewhere halfway between the

two : it is dominated—but less dominated—by the
revolver than that of Stephen Crane, and dominated,
but less dominated, by the moral scruple than that of
James.   But the approach to life is the same with all
these three : they show you that disillusionment is to
be found alike at the tea-table, in the slum and on
the tented field.   That is of great service to our
Republic.

Anglo-Saxondom—the world—is too full of propagandists who cry, on the one hand, that Utopia
is only to be found in the cultural conditions of
drawing-rooms thinly veneered with a knowledge
of the more conventional polite letters ; on the other
hand, there are too many who cry that virtue is the
property of those alone who wear the red badge of
courage—who are scarred by the wars or gnarled by
combat with the sea in winter.   Or again others will
tell you that true heroism resides in the foundries
alone—or in Slums. . . . The probability is that
Heaven on Earth is to be found only in the kind
hearts of kindly men who have known disillusionment.   And it is towards that discovery that the
writers who are in the mainstream of literature help
and have helped humanity.   That is *their* service to
the Republic.

Their preoccupations are not with that service :
though from time to time they will look and claim
that acknowledgment.   That is the meaning of the
saying that every true work of art has a profound
moral significance.   So they talk rather of "technique"
which is a handy word, than of "healing waters of
thought," of "fair gardens of invention"—or even
of "distant prospects."

It occurs to me that I have given a picture of

Henry James in which small personal unkindlinesses
may appear to sound too dominant a note. That is
the misfortune of wishing to point a particular
moral. I will not say that loveableness was the
predominating feature of the Old Man : he was too
intent on his own particular aims to be lavishly
sentimental over surrounding humanity. And his
was not a character painted in the flat, in water-
colour, like the caricatures of Rowlandson. For
some protective reason or other, just as Shelley used
to call himself the Atheist, he loved to appear in the
character of a sort of Mr. Pickwick—with the rather
superficial benevolences, and the mannerisms of
which he was perfectly aware. But below that
protective mask was undoubtedly a plane of nervous
cruelty. I have heard him be – to simple and quite
unpretentious people—more diabolically blighting
than it was quite decent for a man to be—for he
was always an artist in expression. And it needed
a certain fortitude when, the studied benevolence
and the chuckling, savouring, enjoyment of words,
disappearing suddenly from his personality, his dark
eyes rolled in their whites and he spoke very brutal
and direct English. He chose in fact to appear as
Henrietta Maria—but he could be atrocious to those
who behaved as if they took him at that valuation.

And there was yet a third depth—a depth of
religious, of mystical, benevolence such as you find
just now and again in the stories that he " wanted "
to write—in the *Great Good Places*. . . . His
practical benevolences were innumerable, astonishing
—and indefatigable. To do a kindness when a sick
cat or dog of the human race *had* " got through " to
his mind as needing assistance he would exhibit all

the extraordinary ingenuities that are displayed in
his most involved sentences. When "poor dear
Stevie" at Brede fell sick of his last, protracted
illness, the personal concern that James showed
was almost fantastic. He turned his days into
long debates over this or that benevolence—and
he lay all night awake fearing that he might have
contemplated something that might wound the
feelings or appear patronising to the sick boy. He
would run the gamut of grapes, public subscriptions,
cheques. He cabled to New York for sweet-corn
and soft-shelled crabs for fear the boy might long
for home-food. And, when they came he threw
them away—for fear they should make him more
home-sick !

Whilst these pages were appearing simultaneously
in the *English Review* and the *Dial* I found myself faced by a dilemma. I wanted to show how
tender and how considerate the Old Man could
be. Yet so many of those to whom he showed
benevolence are still alive, prosperous now and apt
to resent being reminded that they ever needed
assistance. On the other hand, I had an instance
of singular tenderness towards myself: if I related
it it might appear like self-glorification, as if I were
attempting to lay claim to a greater share in the Old
Man's thoughts than I have any desire to claim: if I
suppressed it I should certainly fall short of justice
to the Master. So I tried both ways, suppressing
it in the *English Review* and trying it on in the
Dial.

Looking at it there, it does not seem so immodest.
I have said that my relation with James was in no
sense literary—and I never knew what it *was*. I am

quite prepared to have some gentleman write to the
papers to say that James repeatedly told him that I
was James's bottle-washer, or toady. But it was not
that. I am perfectly sure that I never in my life
addressed to the Master one word of praise or of
flattery and, as far as I know, he called me *le jeune
homme modeste* and left it at that. He did indeed
confess to having drawn my externals in Morton
Densher of the *Wings of the Dove*—the longish,
leanish, looseish, rather vague Englishman who,
never seeming to have anything to do with his days,
occupied in journalism his night hours.

I may as well now confess that in drawing Henry
VIII in one of my own novels I was rendering the
Master in externals—and mighty life-like the Press
of those days found the portrait to be. . . . I dare
say, anyhow, that he took me to be a journalist of a
gentle disposition, too languid to interrupt him.
Once, after I had sent him one of my volumes of
poems, he just mentioned the name of the book,
raised both his hands over his head, let them slowly
down again, made an extraordinary, quick grimace,
and shook with an immense internal joke. . . . Shortly
afterwards he began to poke fun at Swinburne.

In revenge, constantly and with every appearance
of according weight to my opinions, though he
seldom waited for an answer, he would consult me
about practical matters—investments now and then,
agreements once or twice—and, finally, unceasingly
as to his fantastic domestic arrangements. He
had at one stage portentous but increasingly un-
satisfactory servants of whom, in his kindness of
heart, he would not get rid until their conduct
became the talk of the Antient Town of Rye.

So, one day he came over to Winchelsea to ask
me if I thought a Lady Help would be a desirable
feature in an eminent bachelor's establishment. . . .
Going as we seemed eternally in those days to be
doing, down Winchelsea Hill under the Strand Gate,
he said :

" H . . ., you seem worried ! " I said that I was
worried. I don't know how he knew. But he knew
everything.

Ellen Terry waved her gracious hand from the
old garden above the tower ; the collar of Maximilian
the dachshund called for adjustment. He began
another interminable, refining, sentence — about
housemaids and their locutions. It lasted us to the
bridge at the western foot of Rye.

In Rye High Street he exclaimed—he was extraordinarily flustered :

" I perceive a compatriot. Let us go into this
shop ! " And he bolted into a fruiterer's. He came
out holding an orange and, eventually, throwing it
into the air in an ecstasy of nervousness and stuttering
like a schoolboy :

" If it's money H . . ." he brought out. " Mon
sac n'est pas grand. . . . Mais puisez dans mon sac ! "

I explained that it was not about money that I
was worried, but about the " form " of a book I was
writing. His mute agony was a painful thing to
see. He became much more appalled, but much less
nervous. At last he made the great sacrifice :

" Well, then," he said, " I'm supposed to be . . .
Um, um . . . There's Mary . . . Mrs. Ward . . .
does me the honour . . . I'm supposed to know
. . . In short: Why not let me look at the
manuscript ! "

I had the decency not to take up his time with it.
. . . Les beaux jours quand on était bien modeste!
And how much I regret that I did not.

The last time I saw him was, accidentally, in
August of 1915—on the fourteenth of that month, in
St James's Park. He said:

"Tu vas te battre pour le sol sacré de Mme. de
Stael!"

I suppose it was characteristic that he should say
"de Mme. de Stael"—and not of Stendhal, or even of
Georges Sand! He added—and how sincerely and
with what passion—putting one hand on his chest
and just bowing, that he loved and had loved France
as he had never loved a woman!

Revisiting now the glimpses of our Moon of
Prose, one finds little trace, alas! of the passage of
this great and good man—nor yet of his love for
France.

PART III

THE BATTLE OF THE POETS

" *Euripides:* I'll show ye, and if you'll point out a Tautology
Or a single word clapp'd in to botch a verse—
That's all !—I'll give you leave to spit upon me ! "

The Frogs.

I

"THOUGHTS BEFORE BATTLE"

I ASK to be taken as writing the pages that follow with some diffidence. When it is a matter of prose I know what I want; I know what I want to say; and I know that I can say what I want to say with some exactness. Prose is for me an instrument— like a tool of precision. But the moment I come to want to write about verse I feel—possibly doubts, possibly misgivings; certainly some of the diffidence of the novice. For I suppose that until lately I had not devoted to the problem of verse any of the close and sedulous thought that gives a man a real right to demand to be listened to on any given subject. I had thought about verse desultorily before 1912; it was not until 1915 or 1916, during the enforced waitings of a life sometimes of rather frenzied action, that I devoted really the whole of my æsthetic mind to the practical side of verse-writing. I made a great number of metrical experiments of my own and thought constantly of the metrical devices that had been adopted by the writers of such works as had given me that high, fine pleasure that poems alone can give. And, since that troubled time, I have continued in the same habits.

I should like to make a confession of faith: I believe the conception—and if possible the writing—

of poetry to be the only pursuit worthy of a serious man, unless the vicissitudes of his time call on him to be also a soldier. I have always held this belief; I have never changed in it; I trust that I never shall. I do not mean to say that there are no other pursuits, professions, callings or avocations that Destiny may not force upon a proper man and he endure them with dignity, honour and an unbent head. . . . But even then, if he does not follow them in the spirit of a poet—and with the self-sacrifice of a soldier—he is not a proper man and I hope I may never have to know him.

But, until the earlier date that I have given above, although I never faltered in this belief, the only writings, at any rate of my own day, that I could call poetry had been in the form of prose, not of verse. When—so very occasionally!—in some of the writings of the present Poet Laureate, of Mr. Walter De la Mare, of Christina Rossetti, of Robert Browning, I came across passages that stirred me with an unmistakable call, it was the prose quality of those passages, not the metrical values, to which I attached importance. It was the simplicity of the wording; it was the beauty of the image evoked by the contact of simple words one beside the other.

Of that earlier time I remember images called up by two living poets. The one rendered distant ships, like silver-points on a grey horizon : that was Mr. De la Mare ; the other made visible the depths of still fresh water, beside the piles of a boating stage—on the Thames, I should say. That was in a poem by Mr. Robert Bridges. I do not mean to say that I cannot remember other passages of these two poets ; I can. I believe I could recite several poems by

each of them, with possibly a verbal error here and
there.

And just, as far as I am concerned, as it is with
these two living poets, so it is with the two dead
ones.   Christina Rossetti was an infinitely great
master of words, but the emotions her work always
gave me were those of reading prose—and so it was
with Browning . . . I have seldom received a greater
stirring of enthusiasm than on the day when—quite
late in life—I first came upon the words, at the end
of the first paragraph of the " Flight of the
Duchess . . .":

And all this is our Duke's Country !

And that is certainly a prose effect and a prose
rhythm.   But isn't it glorious ? . . .   So that, only the
other day, I surprised myself by saying to Mr. Pound,
the words coming out from some subconscious depths
where I did not know that the opinion lay : " After
all—the only English poet that matters twopence is
Browning ! "   I don't know what Mr. Pound
answered ; I very seldom do know what Mr. Pound
answers ; but he did not knock me down, so that
I dare say he was substantially in agreement with
myself . . .

I will try to make clear how this progression of
effect has taken place in my thoughts.   I was unconscious that it had taken place, as I have said ; but the
idea having, as it were, reported itself for duty, I can
trace its genesis.   I trust I may be allowed to repeat
myself—I mean to repeat ideas that I have already
put into print.   I never came across any trace that
any human soul had ever read any of my former
critical writings ; by certain reverberations I can now

tell that I have some readers, so I will again make the statement that for a great nnmber of years I could not read "poetry." I wanted to ; but I could not. I used to put that down to the fact that rhymes, accents, stresses, assonances, alliterations, vowel colourings, and the other devices of poets, embarrassed me as a reader. But this was not the case. . . . The real fact is that—the dog it was that died.

I have discovered this for myself from my own practice in verse. I found that as soon as I came to write a " poem " I automatically reduced my intelligence to the level of one purely childish. And, looking one day through the Collected Edition of my own poems that some misguided publisher issued some years ago and that no soul appeared to purchase or read—looking them through again, then, I was appalled to observe that in the whole affair there were not twenty lines that, had I been writing prose, I should not have suppressed. . . . Everything ; every single group of words was what in French is called *chargé* . . . It was not so much that the stuff was rhetorical ; it had not the marmoreal quality of true rhetoric—the kind that one finds on tombstones. It was just silly—with the silliness of a child of a bad type.

Heaven knows I cannot re-read my own prose with anything but mortification—but it is a mortification proceeding rather from the eternal sense of failure that every conscious artist must feel all his life unless he has a good bottle of wine beneath his waistcoat. . . . One has had ideals and has fallen short. That is gloomy enough. But when I read my own verse I know that I have *tried* to write like a brandified sentimentalist.   And I have succeeded every time. . . .

Now, why is this ?   I can assure the reader that alcoholism has very little to do with it.   And I think I can give the answer.   It is simply that every poet —until lately every poet—the moment he takes pen in hand in order to write, say, a sonnet or a triolet or decasyllables, rhymed or unrhymed, at once begins to " write down."   This was the case originally, simply because rhyme and metre were difficult things and an indulgent, primitive Public made allowances. Nowadays the writing down has become a habit, a fashion, a necessity—and a less primitive, less indulgent public can no longer be got to listen to Verse at all.   At any rate, there is hardly a poet of to-day or yesterday who ever, in his matter, his ideas and his verbal texture, attempts to soar above the level of the intellect of scarcely adolescent pupils in young ladies' seminaries—hardly ever a poet who, in his verse, attempts to render a higher type of mentality than that to be found in a Grimm's Fairy Tale. . . . Or it might be more just to say Hans Andersen ; for, as far as I can remember, Andersen was more of a snob than Grimm.

Poets in fact, once they put on their laurel crowns, divest themselves of every shred of humour, irony, or incisive knowledge of life as it is lived.   I can hardly think of any save Heinrich Heine, Browning—and sometimes Christina Rossetti—who were born since 1790 and did not consider verse-writing as something aloof from life, art, form and language.   I will put the matter as a parable : the facts that follow are not exactly what happened.   One must slightly obscure facts when one is writing of one's contemporaries.

But the truth of this parable to the Spirit of the Age is irrefutable.

There were in the City of London, then, two eminent *littérateurs*. . . . Let us call them Messrs. X. and Y. Both were men of brains, humour, and of a sufficient adroitness to have made for themselves comfortable careers—this last being no easy task and one which must have made them acquainted with a considerable surface of such life as is lived in what Henry James used to call the *bas fonds* of journalism. . . . A pretty mean life. . . . But, in an evil hour, each of these gentlemen conceived the idea of writing Verse on a large scale. One—Mr. X.—produced a play in rhyme. Mr. Y. replied with a slice of an epic.

Each was a Reviewer! Mr. Y. reviewed his colleague's verse drama, writing a sort of paraphrase of Sheridan's *Critic*—the Spanish Fleet Mr. X.'s heroine could not have seen because it was not yet in sight, and so on. Mr. X. reviewed the instalment of the epic, in the style of Macaulay's review of Satan Montgomery. He pointed out that it is contrary to natural principles to write

> Thus to its goal the aspiring soul doth mount
> As streams meander level with their fount,

or words to that effect. We were, in fact, presented with the inspiring spectacle of a controversy in the good old style of *The Edinburgh* versus *The Quarterly Reviews*. That, of course, is nothing. Some one in England is always trying to drag literature back to those days and that tone. The point was that Mr. X. concluded his review by saying that, though he had, regretfully, pointed out some of the innumerable absurdities contained in Mr. Y.'s epic, nevertheless Mr. Y. was to be congratulated on revealing his real personality in his work—an exhibition of courage rare in the poets of to-day; Mr. Y., at the end of his review, stated that though he had regretfully pointed out some of the innumerable imbecilities contained in his *confrère's* poetic drama, Mr. X. was to be congratulated on his rare courage in revealing his true personality in his poem. . . . And, since each gentleman had called the other's work a product of an imbecile mind, that was hitting below the belt !

As I read the portents of our moonlit heavens, these two—quite imaginary—gentlemen will be united on one point—they desire to drive out of Literature Mr. Pound, Mr. Flint, and most of my favourite poets. And I beg the reader to believe that hardly anything would have dragged me back into the Literary Life from which I had taken a quite sincere farewell but the desire to prevent this infamy and this disaster.

II

I concluded the first part of this survey by lightly, and, I trust, good-humouredly, grazing the subject of Les Jeunes, who were quite young in the Season of 1914. I fancy the frame of mind of myself and the others who welcomed these then eccentric creatures was one of gentle bewilderment as to their products combined with an absolute confidence in the genius of the various young men whom we backed. I may point out again that I come of a family that, for generations, has impoverished itself in combating Academicism and in trying to help—

geniuses. . . . So I may claim to have in the blood
the tic of combating Academicism and the hope of dis-
covering new, beautiful talents—and, I trust, the
faculty of absolute indifference to my personal fate
or the fate of my own work.

Thus I profess to a certain inherited *flair* for—
a certain sense that it is a duty to forward—the
recognition of young men with, to change the idiom,
individualities, practising one or other of the arts.
And towards the end of Marwood's and my career
in control of the *English Review*, he and I and the
few friends who were interested in a real revival of
Literature began to feel that life was worth living. . . .
There appeared on the scene—I place them in the
order of their appearance, as far as I can remember—
Mr. Pound, Mr. D. H. Lawrence, Mr. Tomlinson,
Mr. Norman Douglas, " H.D.," Mr. Aldington, Mr.
Flint—and afterwards some Americans— Mr. Frost,
Mr. T. S. Eliot, Mr. Edgar Lee Masters. And of
course there were Gaudier Brzeska and Mr. Epstein.
It was—truly—like an opening world. . . .

It was like an opening world. . . . For, if you
have worried your poor dear old brain for at least a
quarter of a century over the hopelessness of finding,
in Anglo-Saxondom, any traces of the operation of a
conscious art—it was amazing to find these young
creatures not only evolving theories of writing and
the plastic arts, but receiving in addition an immense
amount of what is called " public support " . . . I do
not think I am exaggerating when I say that, at any
rate for the London Season of 1914, these young
fellows not only drove the old—oh, the horribly wearisome!—Academics out of the field, the market, and the
forum ; they created for themselves also a " public "

that had never looked at a book otherwise than to be
bored with it ; or considered the idea that an Art
was an interesting, inspiring, or amusing appearance.
That was extraordinarily valuable. And I believe
that their influence at that date extended across the
Atlantic itself and that there it still obtains.

We Anglo-Saxons are the mock of the world ;
there is no nation that does not despise us for our
commercial ideals, our incredible foreign politics—and
the complete absence of any art as a national characteristic . . . The Dutch have their painters ; the
Flemings have their down-to-the-ground poets of
mysticism ; the Germans have their Romantic music ;
their Grimmish lyrics. The French have everything.
The Siamese have their beautiful pots ; the Russians
—again, possibly everything.|| The Poles have im-
mense rhetorical gifts ; the Zulus their folk song ; the
Irish their Historic Sense, which is an art too. We
have nothing, and there is no race in the world that
does not point the finger of scorn at us.

That is the lamentable fact. But in 1914 Les
Jeunes had succeeded in interesting a usually un-
moved but very large section of the public—and had
forced that public to take an interest not in the stuff
but the methods of an Art. The Cubists, Vorticists,
and the others proclaimed that the plastic arts must
be non-representational ; the Imagistes, Symbolistes,
who joined up, I think, with Vorticism, proclaimed
the immense importance of the "live" word—the
word that should strike you as the end of a live wire
will, if you touch it. Actually, I fancy that the
main point of their sympathy and contact was their
desire to impress on the world their own images.
Or, let us put it that the first point of their doctrine

would be that the artist should express by his work his own personality.

Let us consider this canon with some seriousness.

The Impressionists—and it was the Impressionists that the Vorticists, Cubists, Imagistes, and the rest were seeking to wipe out—the Impressionists in the plastic or written arts had been the leaders of the Movement that came immediately before these young fellows. And the main canon of the doctrine of Impressionism had been this : The artist must aim at the absolute suppression of himself in his rendering of his Subject. You were to see as little as possible of the image of M. Courbet in a Courbet; you were to see nothing at all of Flaubert when you read *Trois Contes*. To look at a painting of willow trees under a grey sky ; to read *Cœur Simple* or *Le Rouge et le Noir*, *What Maisie Knew* or *Fathers and Children*, was merely to live in the lives and the minds of Felicité, Mrs. Wicks, whose constant dread was that she might be "spoken to," or of Bazarov . . . Above all the reader was to receive no idea of the figures of Stendhal or his followers . . . For Impressionism begins with Henri Beyle who wrote as Stendhal.

Let me—since even the first commandment of Impressionism is probably unfamiliar to the Anglo-Saxon reader—repeat this formula in another image. That is bad Art ; but I hope to be pardoned by the shades of my Masters. Is the Reader, then, conversant with the Theory of Podmore's Brother ? . . . Podmore's Brother was accustomed to perform certain tricks on members of the public whilst so holding their attentions that they were quite unconscious of his actions. He talked so brilliantly that whilst his tongue moved his hands attracted no attention. It is not a very difficult trick to perform . . . If the Reader will give a box of matches to a friend and then begin to talk really enthrallingly, he will be able to take the box of matches from his friend's hands without his friend being in the least conscious that the matches have gone. Closing his discourse, he will be able to say to his friend : " Where are the matches ? "—and the friend will not have any idea of their whereabouts . . . It is a trick worth performing —the tongue deceiving the eye . . .

It is a trick worth performing—because it is the Trick of Impressionism—the Impressionist writer or painter telling his story with such impressiveness that the Reader or the Observer will forget that the Impressionist is using pen or brush ; just as your suppositious Friend, lost in your conversation, forgets that you take the matches from his hands . . .

The Cubists, Vorticists, Imagistes, Vers Libristes, who in 1914 seemed about to wash out us Impressionists, said simply : " All this attempt to hypnotise the Public is mere waste of time. An Artist attracts ; gets a Public or royalties from sales because he is a clever fellow. Let him begin by saying : 'I am a clever fellow . . . ' And let him go on saying : ' What a fellow I am ! ' Conspuez the Subject ! A bas all conventions of tale-telling ! We, the Vorticists, Cubists, Imagistes, Symbolists, Vers Libristes, Tapagistes are the fine, young Cocks of the Walk ! We and we only are the Playboys of the Western World. We and we only shall be heard " . . . They came very near it.

I remember well a walk I took once with one of my young geniuses on one side of me and Mr. Pound

on the other . . . Of what Mr. Pound talked, I have
no idea. He was expressing himself, in low tones, in
some Transatlantic dialect. This Genius, however,
was plain to hear.

"What is the sense," he said, " of all this '*justifi-
cation*' of a subject that Maupassant and you and
Conrad indulge in . . . You try to trick the reader
into believing that he is hearing true stories . . . But
you can't . . . Maupassant takes three hundred words
out of a two-thousand-word conte to describe a
dinner party with a doctor at it . . . And the doctor
tells a story . . . Or Conrad takes twenty thousand
words out of an immense novel to describe a public-
house on the river at Greenwich . . . In order to
'*justifier*' his story . . . It is a waste of time . . .
What the public wants is Me . . . Because I am not
an imbecile, like the component members of the
public ! . . ."

I dare say he was right . . . At any rate our
Public took *Blast*; Signor Marinetti and his
immense noises, his lungs of brass; Mr. Epstein and
his Rock Drill, with great seriousness and unparalleled
avidity . . . And I was so much a member of the
Public that I determined—very willingly, for I always
detested writing—to shut up shop. I said to myself :
" I will write one more book ! "—a book I had been
hatching for twelve years. " And then no more at
all ! " . . . So the Vorticists and the others proceeded
on their clamorous ways . . . They abolished not
only the Illusion of the Subject, but the Subject itself
. . . They gave you dashes and whirls of pure colour ;
words washed down till they were just Mr. Pound's

Petals on a wet black bough !

Signor Marinetti shouted incredibly in the Doré

Gallery, and a sanguinary war was declared at the Café Royal between those youths who wore trousers of green billiard cloth and whiskers and those who did not . . . The Cabaret Club was raided by the Police, and found to be full of the wives and aged mothers of Cabinet Ministers . . . The Academic writers of the *Literary Journal*, with their incredibly dull snufflings about the placket-holes of Shelley's mistresses, paled till they had the aspect of the posters of yesterday on the walls of the year before last . . .

Alas! that was in 1914 . . . To-day they are all back again in the saddle and the gobbling noises about the tuberculous lungs of Keats,—a beautiful user of words who, had Destiny not been as remorseless to his poor shade as in life she was to his racked body, would have escaped the attention of these stamp collectors—the gobbling noises about the lungs of Keats, the immense, long articles about the orthography of Shakespeare's Fourth Folios, the voluminous disquisitions on the poetasters from whom Scott derived his chapter headings—all these incredibly uninteresting matters have once more killed the interest of the Public in the Arts . . . For what, to the Public, is Fanny Brawne?

I will put the matter in another parable, the facts being this time true . . .

The wife of my headmaster once said to me—I was revisiting my school, and she was looking at a *Literary Journal* that I had brought down—once said, looking musingly over the top of the paper:

" ' Love letters of John Keats to Fanny Brawne, edited by Buxton Forman.' " She was reading the title of a review. And she went on to ask: " Who *was* Keats ? "

I said :

> " A thing of beauty is a joy for ever . . . "

And immediately she continued :

> " Its loveliness increaseth ; it shall never
> Pass into nothingness . . . "

It was not, that is to say, that the lady was closed to or ignorant of the beauty of Keats—it was simply that the *Literary Journal* was so intolerably wearisome that she knew nothing of the sort of ana that . . . But perhaps I am saying too much.

II

MR. POUND, MR. FLINT, SOME IMAGISTES OR CUBISTS, AND THE POETIC VERNACULAR

"Language.

"Use no superfluous word, no adjective which does not reveal something.

"Don't use such an expression as 'Dim lands of peace.'* It dulls the image. It mixes an abstraction with the concrete. It comes from the writer's not realising that the natural object is always the *adequate* symbol.

"Go in fear of abstractions. Do not retell in mediocre verse what has already been done in good prose. Don't think any intelligent person is going to be deceived when you try to shirk all the difficulties of this unspeakably difficult art of prose by chopping your composition into line lengths . . .

"Be influenced by as many great artists as you can but . . . don't allow 'influence' to mean merely that you mop up the particular decorative vocabulary of some one or two poets whom you happen to admire. . . .

"Let the neophyte know assonance and alliteration, rhyme immediate and delayed, simple and polyphonic as a musician would expect to know harmony and counterpoint and all the minutiæ of his craft. No time is too great to give to these matters or to any one of them, even if the artist seldom have need of them. . . ."

So speaks Mr. Pound in his *Retrospect*—he, too, "Revisiting"—from *Pavanes and Divisions.*†

* This expression appears in the first piece of pure Vers Libre that I (F. M. H.) ever wrote—in 1895, I think.
† *Pavanes and Divisions*, June, 1918, pp. 97–99.

AND these rules are very excellently put and thought out : I wish I had Mr. Pound's knack of cutting the heart out of a subject. They have, however, the disadvantage of being written for the Instructed. Let me attempt to explain how they came about.

The least Instructed of readers is probably sensible of the fact that for, let us say, eighty years or so, there has been in existence in these Islands a peculiar jargon which we may as well agree to call the Poetic Vernacular. This provincial dialect has nothing to do with any living, practicable or spoken speech. It is not necessarily meant to convey anything connected with life ; it is a sort of blended product of industry and pruriency. Perhaps its nature is best expressed in this way : There is now a poet—I think it is Mr. Aldous Huxley, and in that case I may as well say that I have a respect for his achievements and still greater expectations for his future —who, I am told, had occasion to state in the course of one of his poems that after a convivial meal in familiar society he sometimes undid his collar stud, or his waistcoat button— something like that. Again, I am told—for I have this story from hearsay alone—that this poem caused more than a ten days' scandal amongst the literati of London. It is, in short, not to be thought of that a collar-stud should make its appearance in verse.

This prohibition applies to most domestic implements, furnishings, and to most garments—but not to all. You might, I mean, write of dishes succulent but not of saucepans ; of waxen candles, not of gasmantles ; of silken petticoats, not of unmentionables. These taboos the Reader will have learned even at school : he will no doubt have written verses towards gaining an " English " prize—or he will have heard

his " English " Master criticising papers of verses by
his schoolmates.   I remember writing, when I was
already a full-fledged Author, for my brother who
was still at school, a free rendering of some lines of
Virgil.   One of them ran :

> " White heifers standing underneath low oaks."

My brother was severely and sarcastically handled
for handing this in.   For the line itself his Master
substituted in blue pencil :

> " The lowing herd, mute 'neath umbrageous boughs ! "

But let us attend at the birth of a Poem of the Great
Tradition.

A certain Poet, slightly of my acquaintance,
desired lately to write a poem to the Pole Star.
This is a very worthy subject for a Poem.   The
Pole Star has shone in its firmamental position for
a long time.   It has been referred to so often in
Verse that it may be said to be a subject assuredly
hallowed by long tradition.   It must be forty years
since some undergraduate, since crowned with laurels,
wrote :

> " See, in the firmament above the Schools,
> The boding constellation of the Plough ! "

And, to a reflective and orthodox mind, it is really
exhilarating and mysterious to consider that the
Pointers always and always align themselves in its
direction, or that it always and always broods over
True North. . . .

Some of the more romantic of these aspects of the
luminary our poet desired to record in verse of the
heroic type.   He left out of his consideration, as
utilitarian, the star's kinship in function to the
prismatic compass.   He wanted mostly to state that

the span of human life is at best but a short thing
compared with the range of the æons during which
the POLE STAR has hung in the heavens and been
unobtrusively useful to denizens of the earth. He
started on his poem and about the fourteenth line
ended on the rhyme "Forest." (He had been
observing the star from St. John's Wood.) Forest is
not a difficult word to find a rhyme for. Our Poet
hit upon "sorest." . . . He wrote then the line :

"When human dole is at his worst and sorest . . ."

This led him into a digression explaining what
are the worst of human misfortunes. He described
frozen widows in the wilds of the Bukhovina ; to
rhyme with that he found it necessary to describe
rapes, arsons, artillery-plasterings, and floods on the
Dwina. . . . This brought him legitimately back to
the theme of the short duration of human life. . . .
His ninety-seventh line ended with the word "long."
To this he found—after dallying with the substantive
"thong," which would of course have let him write a
great deal about the use by sledded Cossacks of the
knout—the rhyme "song." So he wrote twenty-
seven lines about Sappho and the Isles of Greece.
His theme was, of course, a very inclusive one ; the
North Star shone on the Lesbian—as it did on Miles
Standish, Ralph Waldo Emerson, the Encyclopædia
Britannica and the late Oscar Wilde. . . . And at line
1602, remembering that so far he had forgotten to
bring the North Star in very often, he wrote :

"So thinking, sitting on the dash-dash ground,
What time the Star sheds dash-dash beams around
I mused and in my dash-dash visionings
Saw mighty pomps of Kaisers (ALTERED TO CAESARS) and of Kings
Proceeding on the dash-dash dash-dash way
Where pale the Pole Star pours his dash-dash ray !"

Our poet then wished to write a poem about the comparative longevity of the North Star. He devoted to this topic eleven lines. The allurements of RHYME, along with the necessity of METRE (he filled in the dash-dash's with appropriate adjectives before sending the MS. to the printers), had caused him to write 1591 lines that were pure digression. . . . Had he limited himself to his eleven lines he might at least have been interesting. Had he written four of VERS LIBRE they might have been immortal—like:

HERAMEN MEN EGO SETHEN ATHI PALAI POTA . . .

That, however, would have been difficult !

But what I particularly wish the reader to observe is our poet's method of filling in his adjectives. Hě had at his disposal, in his ear, most of the epithets of Keats, Shelley, Coleridge, Marlow of the mighty line, the *Euphues* of Lily, Malory, Swinburne, and Rossetti ; he knew that, by the rules of the game he must use no word not employed by one or other of these writers. He refreshed, therefore, his mind. Taking a copy of *The Eve of Saint Agnes*, he found at the second line, the adjective "frozen." He had contemplated himself as thinking his thoughts in the early summer : but the Pole Star after all is the North Star and Shakespeare has written of the "frozen North." Remembering later, however, the adjective dædal as applied by Shelley to the Earth, in the *Hymn of Pan*, our friend substituted the latter word. From Shelley, too, he at first took "multitudinous" for his visionings ; but he remembered that he needed at this juncture a dissyllable, and he substituted "gloom-pleased" from *To Sleep*. From the *Morte d'Arthur* which is disconcertingly lacking in adjectival felicities, or indeed from adjectives at all, he derived the compound Jesu-Camelot, the collocation suggesting that the Caesars and the Kings were led, by the Redeemer, through the dusk to Camelot, there to await their various second comings. That was enormously in the Great Tradition.

The beams and the ray of the Star gave our poet a great deal of trouble. However, chancing to took at the *Last Sonnet* of Keats, he came upon the line:

"Bright Star, would I were steadfast as thou art!"

and so his penultimate adjective was settled. His other one I forget. I think it was "Hushëd"— —a word used by Swinburne, Rossetti, and Thomas the Rhymer.

To save the reader trouble I give the last lines in their completed form:

"So thinking, sitting on the dædal ground,
What time the Star sheds steadfast beams around
I mused and in my gloom-pleased visionings
Saw mighty pomps of Caesars and of Kings
Proceeding on the Jesu-Camelot way
Where pale the Pole Star pours his hushëd ray."

That, then, was how all poems were written until quite lately; indeed, I am told that in the best circles that is how they are still written. . . . The author compiled for his own use a Thesaurus of well-worn, obsolescent words, fit for drawing-room employment: some of these he wrote down in a note-book; others he confided to his memory so that they became part of a poetic vernacular that he never used in conversation or even in correspondence. And he was confident —and indeed the Critics so assured him—that he was following in the footsteps of a great tradition. He was. But he found no readers.

It was to prevent the writing of such poems that the Imagistes, Cubists, Vorticists, other absurdly labelled young men, and Mr. Flint and Mr. Pound, set out in, say, 1911. Their still higher aim was to bring Poetry back into some tune with the real life of the day—to derive it and to return it again to Our People.

That they mostly wrote Vers Libre is not for the moment to the point. What is, is that they all possessed individualities and that their individualities, once their " formula " of the " live " word had been pronounced, forced them to use words with an extreme scrupulosity. . . .

I ask the Reader to believe that the whole question of Language is one of extreme difficulty—and of extreme importance. French critics, who really *know* something about words, have long since pointed out that French words are perfectly clear, defined and disciplined materials—like the tesseræ of a mosaic. Our words, on the other hand, have each a blurred edge—some one has called it an aura. It would be more exact perhaps to call this aura the initial softening of decomposition. For the French poet is continually thinking of the exact sense of a word—the English is for ever haunted by the word's associations. As far as I am concerned, I hold no personal brief for French Verse—that may soothe the agitated patriotic breast! There is for me, a small amount of extremely beautiful French Vers Libre, but French formal verse I have always found absolutely unreadable. It is more sterilised by its conventions than is the usual English formal verse by its

traditionalisms. Nevertheless it is nearer to the popular
life of France, simply because its substance, depending
on its word-meanings, is more comprehensible. You
might put it that Keats is more beautiful to the
connoisseur of obsolescent verbiage than ever Musset
could be to any one—but Musset, or even the
Parnassiens, can be read with a high poetic pleasure
not only by Academicians but by *marchands des
quatre saisons*—costermongers who have never read
a word of Ronsard or Villon.

A language, in fact, is never a dead thing as long
as it is used. Even mediæval Latin continually grew
with the needs of its day, and those countries in which
written language tends to become the close-preserve
of an Intelligentsia are the countries which go towards
barbarism, simply because beautiful thoughts are
removed from the life of the day. And, constantly,
a war has been waged between the inventors and
advocates of new words and those who desire to
standardise the language. If you read Hookham
Frere's *Quarterly Review* of Mitchell's Aristophanes,
you will find Frere—and in the *Quarterly !*—advocating the use of slang. You will find Aristophanes
making fun of the stilted diction of Euripides. The
quarrel is an eternal one.

For myself, I have always tended to the use of
slang, even in passages of gravity, when slang would
express a fine shade that could only otherwise be
put in a great number of sanctioned words. (I will ask
the reader to believe that I am at least as well
acquainted with obsolete words as any Parnassian
poet: that is only a matter of memory.) But humanity,
as the immense ages roll on, develops new senses
and new faculties : it is obvious that our nerves and

senses to-day are things very different from those that distinguished the Victorians. Or, to put the matter at its extremest, the Greeks appear to have thought that the sea was the same colour as wine, whereas we, even the most barbarous of our individuals, are progressing further and further towards the perception of new shades. And slang, very frequently, is the mutinous effort of some free, barbarian spirit, to express a difficult truth. I don't know, innovating purist that I am, that I shall ever bring myself to use the phrase "not half" in verse or in grave prose—and yet I should find it not half difficult to define the exact degree, quantitative or commendatory, that "not half" expresses. Dr. Johnson, on the other hand, said that the man who would use the word "commence"—which in his day was slang —was a scoundrel who would cut his mother's throat. The really gifted writer would, I suppose, be the man who could perceive, prophetically, what new words of his day were destined to remain fresh in the ear.

But a gentleman who gets his vocabulary exclusively, like our friend the Poet of the Pole Star, from the works of poets deceased, is really trying to blunt the perception of his day. That, at any rate, is the effect of his activities ; his motives may be more praiseworthy. And Culture—the word must be restored to its place in our language—is never a matter of limitations to parlour atmospheres : it is really one of discoveries that will show us how new classes of actions may be performed in common and inoffensively. You are not progressively highly cultured if you insist on having your food brought to table in dishes succulent : you are if you use casseroles. You are more cultured because your food

comes better to table—cooking being also an art—
and because you save your servants some of the distasteful work of washing up, kindliness being the
chief point of Culture.

As with actions so with language. The poet who
persists in and the critic who applauds the somnolent
practice of collecting dead words may well say that
he is playing for safety and being comparatively in-
offensive. That is true. He may go further and
aver that parlour games are rare and needful : that
also is true. But where he becomes a national, a
universal, danger is in his claim to the predominance
of the world of Thought for his dead words and
dulling mental processes.

For it must not be forgotten that the mere use
of a word by a great, dead master, tends to kill that
word ; and that is still more true of phrases. Who
to-day could write of the witching hour of night ?
Shakespeare and the Authorised Version killed the
forms of Elizabethan English ; Johnson, Pope, and
Dryden make it impossible for us to write like the
writers of the eighteenth century ; Keats, Shelley,
Beddoes, Darley, and Clough killed Tennyson,
Rossetti, Swinburne and all nineteenth-century verse-
writers except Browning and Christina Rossetti in
her minute felicities—and killed them before they
were even born. I do not mean that the works of
Shakespeare, Pope, and Keats are dead ; but they
exhausted their veins so completely that the human
mind untired cannot without boredom contemplate
further exercises in those manners. The perpetually
—the born-tired mind can, on the other hand, contemplate nothing else, for fear of being startled from
complacency.

In the matter of language at least, first Browning and then Mr. Hardy, showed the way for the Imagiste group—Browning dragging in any old word from an immense, and Mr. Hardy doing the same thing from a rather limited, vocabulary. There is no one living with an affection greater than mine for the poetry of Mr. Hardy: the *English Review* is alive to this day to testify to it. So that I need not be taken as belittling this great poet if I say that for me his vocabulary always seems to have been taken from a country newspaper—from one of those good country newspapers of the forties when the editors were scholars and gentlemen, with here and there an article from Cobbett and with leaders ornamented with quotations from Tully. But Browning, an immense and buoyant personality, simply threw his immense ranges of syllogisms about as a lusty child splashes in the water of his bath.

The value, however, of Browning and the very great value of Mr. Hardy are not essentially vocabulary values—they are values of form. For, in Verse, there is of course a Verse-form to be considered in addition to the architectonics of the novelist. You may say that every lyric—and indeed every Sonnet—is really a short story ; and the reason for the intolerably dull effect produced by nearly all modern and semi-modern verse is simply that the poet as a rule considers himself too important a person to descend to the technique of the creative prose writer. He will not condescend to tell his story in the most effective way simply because he imagines that as soon as he labels himself " poet " he may discard the sublunary consideration of interesting his Reader. As a matter of fact, if you arrogate to yourself the title of poet and claim that, let us say, a poet is to a story-teller as is a barrister to an attorney—the member of a more technically learned profession—you ought to have at least the skill of the lower members of the lower branch. You ought at least to be able to manage your " story " as well as a Paris feuilletonist or a far Western raconteur. That Browning and still more Christina Rossetti conscientiously attempted, and that Mr. Hardy almost always triumphantly performs. That, indeed, is why Mr. Hardy is so infinitely more important as a verse-poet than as a prosateur. . . .

But that quite apart, there remains the question of verse-form. In that, too, these poets showed the way. Mr. Chesterton, in his very excellent monograph on Browning, points out that Browning was almost the first amongst poets to invent a new verse form— or at any rate to attempt to invent a new verse form —for each of his varying mental phases. In that he was trying to get nearer to an expression of his immense personality. For her smaller personality Christina attempted to do the same thing and, inasmuch as she was more conscious of her limitations and had a more scrupulous sense of words, when she succeeded she was much more consummate than the author of *Red Cotton Nightcap Country*.

This New Tradition was carried much further by Mr. Hardy. I am not, of course, claiming Mr. Hardy as an Imagiste, still further am I from suggesting that he is unlearned or ignorant of formal verse, accents, stresses, and what is called prosody. He has made his Imitations; his Sapphic fragments; his renderings of Catullus. The writer of

Change and chancefulness in my flowering youthtime,
Set me sun by sun near to one unchosen ;
Wrought us fellow-like and despite divergence,
      Friends interlinked us . . .

cannot be called either unlearned, unclassical, nor yet
revolutionary.   Yet, as time went on, and this great
poet gave his attention less and less to story telling
and more and more to intimate self-expression, his
versification became, not so much more irregular, but
more rough ; until, if you read the *Sunday Morning
Tragedy*, it is much more the suggestiveness of
simple words grouped in twos and threes that matters
than any smoothness in the lines.   In fact, you may
say that Mr. Hardy's charm of to-day—his power to
excite—is that his writing is no longer a matter of
vowel-colouring and line-units—for he simply takes
his lines by the throat and squeezes them until they
become as it were mutinously obedient ; it is a
matter of mood-colouring and grouped-word units
set anywhere in, or overlapping, the line.   The
tendency becomes more apparent if you contrast the
evolution of Mr. Hardy with that of Mr. Bridges.
For you may say that Mr. Bridges began as a
searcher for, or at any rate a producer of, quiet *mots
justes*, not enormously metricised ; whereas to-day
he searches for only such words as will fit into
classical " feet," not essentially troubling about either
the mood or the expressiveness of the words.

I ought, no doubt, to include the names of many
other verse-poets if I wanted to make this a complete
history of literature in, say, this century.   I ought, in
that case, to dwell on the verse, the vocabulary and
the charm of Mr. De la Mare, whose work, as I have
said, I read constantly and with private delight.   It
is not, I ask the reader to believe, want of generosity

that prevents my doing this—it is merely the fact that I have passed most of my life in search of illustrations of a tendency, and that I am now, as well as I can, giving the reader those illustrations. If I wished to be inclusive I should have two books to write, after the fashion of Mr. Monro's précis of Contemporary Poets. With that work I am substantially in agreement, and the reader interested in the matter might well read that book as an appendix to this one. I can't help the fact that Mr. Monro speaks favourably of my own attainments: it may colour my views: I don't know. One is bound to be in or of a School, as this world goes, and one must take one's praise or blame as one gets it.

And, as long as one gets one's blame for the fact that one belongs to one's tendency and not merely for private reasons, I do not see that one should grumble; or as long as one is omitted because one does not seem to a critic to make a good illustration. The tendency is the thing—and the only thing. It was the tendency, not praise of individuals that gave us once the Border ballads, the plays of Shakespeare, and the poems—not the bibliographies—of Keats and Shelley. We are, in fact, in ships, in great galliasses, or liners, and, whether we like it or not, we cannot paddle individual canoes very far across the immeasurable Ocean. For myself, to change the simile, I am journeying through a rather thick undergrowth, in search of, say, the genus FRINGIL-LAGO. . . . Not then being intent on eagles, nightingales or thrushes, I possibly unduly neglect them as far as the great Scale of Things is concerned. But that is, I hope, preoccupation rather than want of generous Catholicity. And what I in the end most

want to express is the great truth that, although
Mr. Kipling is perfectly right when he says that
there are five and thirty ways of inditing tribal lays,
each one of them being a Valid Form, yet for each
subject and for each mood there is only one—one
only—best possible way !

These things, too, may be said to have been in
the minds of the group that I will call from now on
the Imagistes.   They began their group-life towards
1912, and with various re-groupings, proclamations,
and I dare say the squabbles proper to the young and
the high-spirited, they continued their more or less
combined activities well into the first year of the late
war.

We may say that what most characterised their
products was a sort of cleanness.   That at least is
what strikes me most on once more looking into the
Imagistes anthology that was published in 1914.
The work is free of the polysyllabic, honey-dripping
and derivative adjectives that, distinguishing the
works of most of their contemporaries, makes nineteenth-century poetry as a whole seem greasy and
" close," like the air of a room.

> The hard sand breaks
> And the grains of it
> Are clear as wine.
>
> Far off over the leagues of it,
> The wind
> Playing on the wide shore
> Piles little ridges
> And the great waves
> Break over it.
>
> But more than the many foamed ways
> Of the sea,
>
> I know him,
> Hermes . . .

That is by H. D.

Over the green, cold leaves
And the rippled silver
And the tarnished copper
Of its neck and beak
Toward the deep black water
Beneath the arches
The swan floats slowly. . . .

That is Mr. Flint.

The rustling of the silk is discontinued
Dust drifts over the courtyard,
There is no sound of footfall, and the leaves
Scurry into heaps and lie still,
And she the rejoicer of the heart is beneath them :
A wet leaf that clings to the threshold.

That is Mr. Pound.

Now that I have cooled to you
Let there be gold of tarnished masonry,
Temples soothed by the sun to ruin
That sleep utterly.
Give me hand for the dances,
Ripple at Philæ, in and out,
And lips, my Lesbian,
Wallflowers that once were flame. . . .

That is Mr. William Carlos Williams.

For purposes of comparison I quote two verses
that the Imagistes annexed for this Anthology :

It rains, it rains,
From gutters and drains
And gargoyles and gables :
It drips from the tables
That tell us the tolls upon grains,
Oxen, asses, sheep, turkeys and fowls,
Set into the rain-soaked wall
Of the old Town Hall.

The mountains being so tall
And forcing the town on the river,
The market's so small
That, with the wet cobbles ; dark arches and all,
The owls
(For in dark rainy weather the owls fly out
Well before four) so the owls
In the gloom
Have too little room
And brush by the saint on the fountain
In veering about. . . .

This Ford Madox Hueffer is, I fancy, more conversational than the other extracts; it has the sound rather of a man talking amiably to just any company. H. D. (Miss Doolittle) and Messrs. Flint, Pound, Carlos Williams—and, indeed, all the other Imagistes —seem to be writing very simple and carefully chosen words, sparingly, for incision on alabaster. But I think the Reader will see that the Imagistes are not merely illiterate, writing easily down the first matter that comes into obscene or revolutionary minds. For that is what my dear old friend the *Morning Post* would have you believe. You cannot, in fact, afford to write just anything for incision on marble.

I am quite ready to concede that " marmoreal " writing is not everything. I am ready even to concede that the style of Flaubert is not everything. I notice that Mr. George Moore has lately gone back on his Master's Master—and largely on account of this quality. Mr. Moore demands, now, a little more effervescence than he can find in the *Trois Contes*. Or perhaps this is only to say that he himself is determined to write with more " snap " in future. Mr. Moore has every right to do so : he is a great artist, and his most petulant pronouncements are interesting. But to Flaubert must be conceded the defects of his qualities. He is not, that is to say, an unserious writer—because he happens to be serious. But no writer can afford to let Flaubert's defects outweigh his immensity of genius—until he himself shall have read *Education Sentimentale* fourteen times, and marked the particular pattern of *that* carpet. But the secret of Flaubert being that he was the greatest moralist and the most passionate-disillusioned

writer of moralities that the world has yet seen, it is
unreasonable to ask that he should be also a Crébillon,
a Voltaire, and a Schnitzler.

You have, in fact, whilst reading *Félicité* or *St.
Julien*, to sit as it were mouse-still in a church : but
the quality of attention is in this world so rarely
demanded of one that, if into it we are coerced, it
cannot but make better men, and better poets, of us.
So that we need not condemn the late Flaubert
because the later poems of Mr. Pound, whilst you
are reading them, may make you fidget as if your
seat were gradually becoming extremely hot.　Genius
takes several forms.

The Reader is now asking himself : " Here is this
fellow dragging in Flaubert again.　Why ?　Flaubert
wrote a ' spicy ' novel called *Madame Bovary*.　What
has he to do with Vorticism ?　He was a writer of
prose ; not a poet."　The last assertion I shall answer
in my next chapter : Mr. Flint has indeed already
much more beautifully and completely answered it in
the exquisite sentence from his preface to *Otherworld* which I honour myself by quoting on the fly-
leaf of this Part.　And, if the Reader will—as he
should—read right through that Preface, omitting of
course one sentence, he will see what a beautiful
thing prose can be made in the hands of a master—
and he will learn what a beautiful thing the English
language is.　And do not believe that that is Poet's
Prose, the unbalanced exgurgitations of a Swinburne
determined to shout a Hugo into the position and
the privileges of a demi-god.　It is just beautiful
English, as still as the pointed towers of Oxford ; as
permanent as a drawing in silver-point.　But had
there been no Flaubert in the world perhaps there

would have been no English prose—no English poem
—of that type.

What Flaubert gave to the world was not merely
one book—nor five or six; it was a whole habit of
mind that is changing the face of the globe.   For
communication between man and man is the most
important, the most beneficent of human gifts—and
just and true communication can only be achieved by
an appallingly serious study of Language. . . . And
do not believe that any literary quality, of whatever
nature, can be achieved without this seriousness.
Read, if Flaubert is too serious for you, the *cochonneries*
of Maupassant—for God knows I am no kill-joy—
and you will find just Flaubert's economy and
appropriateness of words, achieved only after the
same seriousness in their study.   You won't, that is
to say, find a phrase that is over-written; you will
not find one that is slipshod.

The vocabulary that we shall ultimately achieve
by the methods of Flaubert and Maupassant—the
vocabulary achieved indeed by the Imagistes—will
be the vocabulary for both the prose and the verse
of the future.   And it will be—as to-day in France
is the case—the vocabulary of the hatter, of the
pharmaceutical chemist, and the policeman, used
over counters, at street corners—and above all in
schools, by the teachers.   Then, indeed, we shall have
a Utopia ! But that day will come only when our
poets have applied to language that furious earnest-
ness which the Bollandist Fathers have used in their
analyses of cases of conscience.

We must, in fact, use in this matter some of the
conscience of the priest even if we are doing no more
than write Revues for the Variety Stage.   I do not

mean that we must recite the poems of Miss Doolittle
from the boards of the Shepherds Bush Empire.
But I do mean to say that, even there, we must
study our audiences until we can give them something at least on the level of—Aristophanes.   Otherwise it will be Movies, Movies, Movies all the way.
That may seem a vulgar saying, but it puts concisely
a very grave fact.   Nemesis in the end overtakes us
all—but it overtakes most terribly the negligent of
mind.   That is why the English verse-poet is to-day
extinct.   In the end the Public depends upon its
writers—upon all its artists—for its place in the
comity of nations.   And a Nation's artists depend—
not materially—but just as absolutely upon its Public.
Homer may have been a beggar, the first singer of
Chevy Chace a cattle-thief, but they drew their
inspiration from, they were beloved by, their own
peoples—and because of them their own peoples are
still beloved in this world of short memories.   It
does not, I fancy, much matter if the Poet starve.
Villon did ; Browning did not.   On the whole, better
poetry would seem to be written by poets who live
in garrets and steal out from time to time to get a
meal in the cafés of some Soho or other, and so die
unrecognised.   That habit of life, at any rate, brings
your poet up against the hard facts of existence and,
usually the harder up a poet is the harder he works
at the quality of his work.   For, as a rule, he soon
learns that " writing down "—most bad popular works
being sincere and he writing with his tongue in his
cheek—leads only to bad writing and not to goodly
cheques.   And whereas the vicious tendency of most
poets, the mental cowardice that leads them to
idealise any other age than their own, is their usual

cause of death, a man brought up against the hard facts of life is apt to regard his own time and his own people with attention. He will be more of a man. I have known a great many poets in the course of my life—these are Reminiscences!—and eighty per cent. of the really fine fellows amongst them had their origins amongst the glamours and squalors of poverty.

Still it matters probably very little how your poet lives. Yet, Recognition, if it be of little consequence, or detrimental, to poets is very necessary to Poetry. It is necessary because poetry can only flourish in an atmosphere of poetry—of contagion. The silly fallacy which has it that poets ought to have large incomes so as to become acquainted with the atmospheres of Grand Babylon Hotels and steam yachts is just a silly fallacy. Any poet who is worth his salt can build in the air better castles than any hotel-keeper and plan better voyages than any millionaire. I do not believe that H. D. has ever, in a floating palace, visited the Isles of Greece, or Mr. Pound, in a Pullman, Cathay. Nevertheless an immense audience is necessary for poetry: without it the poet will not recognise what is his responsibility nor yet will the public accord to him the little indulgences that he must have.

The increasingly miserable condition of poetry in the Western World is due firstly and originally to the obscurantism of the Intelligentsia: but it is due secondly and immediately to sheer want of recognition. These things act in a vicious circle. For it is the merest nonsense to say that any poet or any poetry has been recognised for two—or, really, for three—hundred years. The Shakespeare-Jonson group lived in a world that was saturated with the poetry of themselves and of their schools whether their hearers could read or not; if you like, you may say that Pope, and finally Byron, were read by all the literates of their day. But what poet of to-day can boast of a reading public of 20,000 readers out of a reading population of forty millions? What poet can boast that he is certain of 2,000? For myself, I used in my time to be as much belauded in the Press as any verse-writer of us all: but I do not believe that any volume of verse by myself has found as many as 200 purchasers. How many complete volumes of Keats have been sold since Adonais died? A million? How many hundreds of millions of Anglo-Saxons, all of them able to read, have gone to the grave since that day? How many readers could Tennyson be sure of? 60,000? I do not believe it.

My own experience has convinced me that the Public has a profound distrust of its literary Advisers. I am not talking merely of my own " sales "—though that is a story striking enough. Had I put upon the market a new toy or a new game and had either of those devices received the attention from the Press that I used to receive, millions of people would have been delighted by those inventions. Or, put the same case for Mr. Hardy and you would have to write tens of millions. . . . This can only mean that the Public believes in its Games Advisers—but that it distrusts, profoundly, its Critics. It feels sure that the books recommended to them by these gentlemen will bore them—because of the Poetic Vernacular, the drawing-room atmosphere, the Tradition. . . . No doubt the Public is sometimes wrong: but—I will elaborate this point later on—it is a very wearisome business seeking for the person of the Sacred Emperor through a wilderness of low Tea-Houses !

The fact is that the Public—Humanity all the world over—has come to be more and more exacting as it has come to be more and more elbowed out from the position of a participator in the Arts.   You cannot expect a Public to stomach the rudenesses such as they are, of the Border Ballads, when it no longer has any hand in the making of *Chevy Chaces.* Still less will it stomach imitation Border Ballads. Heine has been born !   Still, still less will it take the recommendations of gentlemen whose sole qualification to speak for literature is having behind them an infinity of mole-work in heaps of unimportant dust. . . .

And do not let the Reader be deluded into thinking that the Commercial Conditions—the paper-and-printers'-wages cry—have anything much to do with it.   The Commercial Conditions of to-day are bitter indeed.   But could our peoples become convinced that the Poetry—the Creative Writing—of this day of ours was really interesting and really founded on the life of the day, really expressed in the words of to-day—and the Commercial Conditions would soon break down.   Bad publishing and cliques of commercial critics can stand as barriers between a languid art and a languid public : they cannot between two vital forces.   The Bad Publisher would go bankrupt, like a hand-cobbler working beside a great Boot Store; the real poet misled by the Intelligentsia would, if he had time, mend his ways. . . . The Commercial Critics—well, they are astute men of business : they would quickly find jobs !

It is, of course, true that men with clear-seeing

minds are often in advance of the level of intelligence of their day. They must wait. I do not expect that, before next Christmas, an enormous public appreciation for Miss Doolittle will arise, or a great demand for the writings of Mr. Pound, Mr. Flint, or Mr. Carlos Williams. The Public very properly demands its time for reflection. The stillnesses of Mr. Flint do not cry aloud with brazen lungs ; the immense, swashbuckling erudition of Mr. Pound needs getting used to. I should, indeed, expect the poems of Miss Sitwell—who is of a quite other school of vivacity, but for whom I have a real admiration—to " come through " far sooner. For I hope I have—but perhaps I have not—made it plain that I have no artistic objection to offer to verbal felicities, tricks and jugglings to " assonances, alliterations, rhymes immediate or delayed, simple or polyphonic "—or else I must rule out Mr. Pound's friend, Arnaut Daniel. And I do not object to human, alive, and whimsical erudition—or else I must rule out Mr. Pound.

For the erudition of the Humanist—from Erasmus to M. Anatole France—is one of the most necessary of qualities. But it must be an erudition that recognises that it itself is of no manner of importance except in so far as it can offer, like a trusty servant, an immense range of human illustration to its Master. It is pleasant to read of half-serious speculations as to the songs of the syrens ; it is delightful to read in *Le Crime de Sylvestre Bonnard* about varying editions and manuscripts of the *Legenda Aurea*. . . . But these are only lights thrown upon the human soul : and such erudition when it is used as a means for obtaining " marks " of one kind or another,

when it is used for the erection of monuments to pro-
vincialisms whether of Goettingen, Cambridge Eng.
or Cambridge Mass.—is the accursed thing that kills
alike true Learning and the love of it.   That for
which Humanity cries out is, not an erudition of
fact, bibliography, or dead words—it is an erudition
that illuminates Life. . . .

For myself, I have always wished that I possessed
some of the immense, human erudition of Mr. Pound.
For the matter of that I have long, gradually, come
to wish that I could put things so well—for then I
could put things so much better.   For Mr. Pound is
a very great poet ; but he approaches prose with the
attack of a writer of dramatic fiction.   He renders,
that is to say, rather than commenting—and the
business of Criticism being comment this gives to his
critical works an atmosphere of restlessness.   So that
his critical writings are much more craftsman's notes
than the balanced or the beautiful prose of the Born
Critic and they are more to be appreciated by—they
will be more useful to—the intelligent Craftsman
than the Uninstructed Reader, however intelligent he
may be.   Compared with the tender, rather muted
and persuasive prose of Mr. Flint, Mr. Pound's harsh
aphorisms are like sharp splinters of granite struck off
by a careless but violent chisel.

But, whatever Mr. Pound is or is not, of this the
Reader may be certain : Wherever two or three
Men of Letters—of Printed Matter—are found united
in irritations some splinters from one or other of Mr.
Pound's chippings will be found at the bottom of
their poor, dear abscesses.   The kindest-hearted man
that ever cut a throat, just as Bertran de Born with
his terrific poems called *Sirventeses* set all Christendom

—all its Princes, Kings, Dukes, and Viscounts at each others' throats and at his, so this American son of all the Troubadours has kept up, has been the storm-centre for, a ceaseless sub-strife throughout distracted Europe. They have ploughed him down and put clods upon his head ; but the Spring comes round again and once more the head, unbowed and not even markedly bloody, rises to grin at our poor old moonbeams. A great vitality : an immense heroism !

And it is a very beautiful heroism—since it has been so persisted in and has remained so without rewards or applause. The uninstructed Reader should imagine this Rufous Terror, with an immense physical vigour and the restless itch of a devil, pursuing the Irritating-Beautiful—in the disguise of a cattle-hand across the Atlantic, in an Islington doss-house, on Montmartre ; as a tramp on the Montagne Noir, in Venice, in Madrid, in Barcelona—and, God knows how, through an infinity of scripts, parchments, Romance notations, volumes, ideographs, libraries, Quellen, documents inédits and the wrappings of fried fish. And of this I am sure : I could not say that I have never written an insincere word " for the sake of a little money or some woman." I do not think I ever have but I don't know. But I will give Mr. Pound that character.

There can have been few men whose deaths have so often been announced.

III

A DESCRIPTIVE INTERLUDE

I do not know why it is that I always figure to myself the Typical Academic Critic of to-day as a youngish, as you might say "thirty-ish," slightly querulous, dark, creaking on the whole Dyspeptic. . . . (The cunning reader will observe that before tiring him with more technicalities I am trying to distract him with one or two thumbnail sketches of combatants in my Batrachomachia. . . . But this is less of a digression than it appears, the hand, like that of Podmore's Brother, attempting to deceive the eye.)

My Typical Academic Critic, then, was born about 1888—sufficient of the late century remaining after his nativity to let his general coloration remain dominantly Victorian. He will wear habitually a dark blue tie, a butterfly collar, a well-brushed dark blue overcoat of Melton cloth, and a bowler hat of unmarked lines. In the drawing-rooms of lady leaders of, let us say the Fabian Society, he will be observed to be looking at Mr. Pound knocking over small tea-tables and whatnots. . . .

At one of the Victorianly founded Public Schools our friend will have begun by founding and editing at a loss the School Magazine. Proceeding to Tuebingen, under the guidance of Professor Wirklicher Geheimrath ——, he obtained his Doctorate for a thesis on the Minor Works of George Crumb. (George Crumb was our past friend the poet who called policemen Thoth and died in a madhouse.) On returning to England he persuaded a leading firm of publishers to issue under his Editorship an edition de luxe, a cheap selection, a cheap completed edition, a bibliography, and a topography, of the Works of that poet. He edited the poet's love-letters and was largely responsible for the not very successful attempt to erect a National Crumb Memorial. This enterprise was interrupted by the war.

By 1912 he was already writing sound articles for the *Literary Journal*, the editor of which periodical considered him to be a model of orthodox erudition, and a most promising young man. By a lamentable oversight he praised a poem called *The Goodly Fere* by Mr. Pound, in 1913. But observing Mr. Pound laughing in the drawing-room of Lady —— he swiftly realised the rashness of this uncalculated action. He announced that Mr. Pound was dead, that very afternoon, to a select circle of young ladies. He continued to write sound articles for the *Literary Journal*.

The war of 1914 in no way interrupted our friend's activities. His knowledge of German being thorough, upon the outbreak of hostilities he obtained a post in the secret service and was instrumental in securing the internment of many suburban aliens. His ready pen, however, rapidly ensured his translation to the Propaganda Branch of that Service—afterwards the Ministry of Information. He here distinguished himself by a series of brilliant exposures of the secret and not so secret vices of Professor Wirklicher Geheimrath —— of Tuebingen. Being transferred to the Press Censorship in Paris, and not knowing the language, he met on the Boulevard Magenta, Mr. Pound, who informed him that Hugo, Lamartine, and Sainte Beuve were no longer leaders of French Literary taste.   Our friend wrote that afternoon for the *Literary Journal*, on whose staff he remained, an article in which he proved that Mr. Pound, Mr. Flint, and Gaudier Brzeska had died of drink—and that French Literature was dead too. . . .

So he pursued his tranquil and honourable career, becoming during the continuance of the struggle, Literary Adviser to three leading publishers, principal shareholder in the Pontardulais and Pwhlelli tinplate works, literary necrologist to three morning newspapers and Chief Reviewer to seven.   On the day after Armistice Day he succeeded to the Editorship of the *Literary Journal*.   To make sure, he signalised this event by writing a leader in which he proved that Mr. Pound, Mr. Flint, Miss Doolittle, M. Paul Fort, M. Henri de Regnier, the Nouvelle Revue, Mr. Quin of New York, and myself were all dead.   This article he called A COUNTRY FIT FOR HEROES.

He had acquired a great taste for Censorship as an occupation and a great distaste for France during his stay in Paris ; for he had acquired some knowledge of the French language and some knowledge of French literature and discovered that Alexandre Dumas père was not highly esteemed as a stylist upon the Boulevards.   Moreover, being overcome with some remorse for his treachery to the Wirklicher Geheimrath ——, his mind executed within him a marked revirement towards the practices and the frame of mind of the spiritual home of Vorschungen.   His articles became therefore weekly apologues upon the bad taste of the French ; he wrote a volume advocating a return to

Tuebingen; pointed out in many corners of the periodical press that unless this last were effected the Intelligentsia of Great Britain must sink beneath the weight of the Income Tax; and kept a vigilant censorial look-out for any young writers who showed in their work any French influences at all.

He became in fact, the Safe Critic of Anglo-Saxon-dom—concealedly, like Giffard of the *Quarterly*, a politician, ready to hound to death any Keats whom he might suspect of being allied to some anti-Court-Party Leigh Hunt or other; and yet ready to kill any new poet, as time went on, with the sneer: This fellow is no Keats.   That is safety play!

Such being the Safe Critic of to-day, it is of course obvious that the woefully small circle of Salons in which literary reputations are now said to be made, can contain no place for gentlemen who stumble over footstools.   The sketch of this personality is of course allegorical—but the truth enshrined is hourly to be recognised, and the Figure dates from All Time.

And this safety-play, using its traditional weapons of personal and æsthetic denigration, comes into its own at a date when the dice, as I have said, are too loaded in favour of the Melton cloth overcoat with the velvet collar and the unpronounced bowler hat. Youth *ought* to go in sombreroes, trousers of green billiard cloth, golden whiskers, with huge cravats, and to be found in cafés if not in hedge alehouses or the cabarets of Montmartre.   Indeed, you might put it that a public which, unconsciously, remembers Villon will believe in no other Youth and so the drawing-rooms are dead.   For, in the Arts, the salons live on the crumbs that fall from the tables of Mont-martre and the Quartier.

I am, believe me, not uttering a pæan in favour of Bohemianism, which is a thing as sterilising as is the drawing-room. It will have dirty cuffs because it is lazy. . . . But, your young artist will have satin rags falling from the lining of his black Inverness because his female companion is too immersed in thoughts of paint tubes to be ready with the needle, and he must have his gaieties and his reunions, inexpensive because he is too immersed himself in his experimental stage to have played for the safety of the *Literary Journal.*

Art is, in short, dependant for its carrying on, for young men making experiments in indigent circumstances, whilst the Typical Critics proclaim their unhonoured deaths and, now and then, knock them on the head. . . . For deaths, there are, alas !

So I give the Reader this little vignette-remembrance of Henri Gaudier—this story of a low teashop. Gaudier, it is true, was a sculptor. He chiselled out of marble and bronze hard lines, precise, enduring forms—not tablets with a few clear words to make an Image. But the one fact is that he is lamentably dead, and the other that he does not happen to practise my own particular art. For I am not, believe me, entirely deficient in a sense of humour, and the fact that in his PREFACE that I quote with such enthusiasm Mr. Flint declares that I am the only Critic in England, that I seldom open an American, Spanish, Basque, or Monegasque Review without finding that Mr. Pound is there declaring that I am one of the only four poets in the world, or that in the Canadian Pacific *Wheatsheaf*, some other of the Jeunes of 1914, declares once a month that I am the only British prosateur—these facts prevent my writing of my friends with that freedom of enthusiasm which I can devote to the memory of a dead sculptor.

And at any rate for a moment in the just-before-the-war days, the Fine, the Plastic and the Literary Arts touched hands with an unusual intimacy and what is called one-ness of purpose. That had nothing to do with any charlatanry—it was the merest modesty. The Sculptors, Painters and Poets and Prosateurs of that Movement happened to synchronise in a discovery. Just as it were when Mr. Flint and Miss Doolittle said to themselves: Keats was a marvellous embroiderer of short stories, let us try to do something else since we shall never do that as well! Mr. Wadsworth and Gaudier said to *them*selves: Rembrandt, Praxiteles, Hogarth, Velasquez, Madox Brown, Courbet and Rodin have very marvellously reproduced solids and lights in two or three dimensions: we shall never do so well: let us try something else!

That was all the charlatanry there was in it— absolutely all. And the Reader should remember that in all the arts—as in all humanity—there exists, deep down and has always existed, at the bottoms of the minds of poets as of aquarellists and ballad writers, the secret ambition to express themselves in abstract Form or in abstract Sound. It is a yearning akin to that of the Lover, the world over—to be loved for himself alone, by sheer force of personality, not for actions, words, physique, kisses or glances. So, for a time at least, the Vorticistes, Cubistes, Imagistes, and Tapagistes united to express themselves in abstractions —just as Father Bach expressed himself in Fugue! There is, in the ambition, perhaps, the fine, the imperishable, impracticability and frenzy of youth—but there is neither charlatanry nor the desire to break up

hearths and homes.   For Politics is usually dragged
into these purely æsthetic matters : you will find fine,
sensible Tory organs; benevolent Cardinal Arch-
bishops; Whig Reviews and Drapers' Gazettes
declaring that the foundations of society are threatened
whenever some Mr. Epstein or other exhibits some
difficult, not obvious cube.   Charles Dickens clamoured
for Governmental action and the imprisonment of
the offenders when my grandfather rendered Our
Lord as washing the feet of Peter in real water and
Millais rendered Him as kissing His mother.   So great
indeed was the then outcry that Millais altered his
figure though my grandfather did not alter his.

All that sort of thing is sheer nonsense, and Cubism
has nothing to do with Bolshevism, except in so far
as Bolshevism is said to have knocked most of its
intelligentsia on the head, thus setting for a groaning
and bored world, an example that the Cubists might
well follow.   But Art has nothing do with Overlord-
ships, Domesticities, the Penal, the Divorce, or the
Property Laws.   It is concerned simply with finding
out the best means of expression between man and
man.   That cannot be said too often.   Vorticism may
have been on a wrong road but it never, in its most
sordid dreams, ever contemplated leading mobs
down . . . Parliament Street !

Anyhow . . . Let me get on with my story of a
low teashop.

I do not know why it is that, when I rehearse in
my ear the cadences of some paragraphs which I wish
to be allowed to write concerning Gaudier, the rhythm
suggesting itself to my mind should be one of sadness.
For there was no one further from sadness than Henri
Gaudier—whether in his being or his fate.   He had

youth, he had grace of person and of physique, he had a great sense of the comic. He had friendships, associates in his work, loves, the hardships that help youth. He had genius and he died a hero. Who could ask for more? Who could have better things?

He comes back to me best as he was at a function of which I remember most, except for Gaudier, disagreeable sensations, embarrassments. It was in late July, 1914: the host—I can't remember who it was—must have been some one I disliked. And I was ordered to be there: the dinner was a parade. I suppose that, even then, I was regarded as the "Grandfather of the Vorticists"—just as *my* grandfather was nicknamed the "Grandfather of the Pre-Raphaelites." Anyhow, it was a disagreeable occasion in an underground haunt of pre-'14 smartness. Do you remember, Gringoire?

And I hate to receive hospitality from a person whom I dislike: the food seems to go bad; there is anyhow a bad taste in the mouth, symbol of a to be disturbed liver. So the band played in the cave that the place was, and there were nasty foreign waiters, and it was late July, 1914. . . . There were also speeches.

Then Gaudier rose. It was suddenly like a silence that intervened during a distressing and reiterated noise. I do not know that I had ever noticed him before except as one amongst a crowd of dirty-ish, bearded, slouch-hatted individuals like conspirators; but, there, he seemed as if he stood amidst sunlight; as if indeed he floated in a ray of sunlight, like the Dove in Early Italian pictures. In a life during which I have known thousands of people, thousands and thousands of people, during which I have grown sick and tired of "people," so that I begin to prefer the society of cabbages, goats, and the flower of the marrow plant, I have never otherwise known what it was to witness an appearance which symbolised so completely—aloofness. It was like the appearance of Apollo at a creditors' meeting. It was sup ernatural.

It was just that. One did not rub one's eyes : one was too astounded ; only, something within one wondered what the devil he was doing there. If he hadn't seemed so extraordinarily efficient, one would have thought he had strayed from another age, from another world, from some Hesperides. One keeps wanting to say that he was Greek, but he wasn't : he wasn't of a type that strayed ; and indeed I seem to feel his poor bones moving in the August dust of Neuville St. Vaast when I—though even only nearly ! —apply to him a name that he would have hated. At any rate, it was amazing to see him there, since he seemed so entirely inspired by inward visions that one wondered what he could be after—certainly not the bad dinner, the attentions of the foreign waiters, a tug at any one's money-bag strings. No, he spoke as if his eyes were fixed on a point within himself ; and yet with such humour and such good humour— as if he found the whole thing so comic !

One is glad of the comic in his career ; it would otherwise have been too much an incident of the Elgin Marbles. But even the heroism of his first, abortive "joining-up" was heroico-comic. As I heard him tell the story, or at least as I remember it, it was like this :

He had gone to France in the early days of the war—and one accepted his having gone as one accepted the closing of a door—of a tomb, if you like.

Then, suddenly, he was once more there. It produced
a queer effect; it was a little bewildering in a bewildering world. But it became comic. He had
gone to Boulogne and presented himself to the
recruiting officer—a N.C.O., or captain, of the old
school, white moustachios, *cheveux en brosse*. Gaudier
stated that years before he had left France without
having performed his military duties, but, since la
patrie was en danger, he had returned like any other
good little piou-piou. But the sergeant, martinet-
wise, as became a veteran of 1870, struck the table
with his fist and exclaimed: " Non, mon ami, it is
not la patrie, but you who are in danger. You are
a deserter; you will be shot." So Gaudier was conducted to a motor-car, in which, under the military
escort of two files of men, a sergeant, a corporal, and
a lieutenant, he was whirled off to Calais. In Calais
town he was placed in an empty room. Outside the
door were stationed two men with large guns, and
Gaudier was told that if he opened the door the guns
would go off. That was his phrase. He did not
open the door. He spent several hours reflecting
that, though they manage these things better in
France, they don't manage them so *damn* well. At
the end of that time he pushed aside the window-
blind and looked out. The room was on the ground
floor; there were no bars. Gaudier opened the
window, stepped into the street—just like that—and
walked back to Boulogne.

He returned to London.

He was drawn back again to France by the
opening of the bombardment of Reims Cathedral.
This time he had a safe-conduct from the Embassy.
I do not know the date of his second joining-up or

the number of his regiment. At any rate, he took part in an attack on a Prussian outpost on Michaelmas Eve, so he had not much delayed, and his regiment was rendered illustrious, though it cannot have given him a deuce of a lot of training. He did not need it. He was as hard as nails and as intelligent as the devil. He was used to forging and grinding his own chisels ; he was inured to the hardships of poverty in great cities ; he was accustomed to hammer and chisel at his marble for hours and hours of day after day. He was a " fit " townsman—and it was " fit " townsmen who conducted the fighting of 1914 when the war was won : it was les parigots.

Of his biography I have always had only the haziest of notions. I know that he was the son of a Meridional craftsman, a carpenter and joiner, who was a good workman, and no man could have a better origin. His father was called Joseph Gaudier—so why he called himself B'jesker I do not know. I prefer really to be hazy ; because Gaudier will always remain for me something supernatural. He was for me a " message " at a difficult time of life. His death and the death at the same time of another boy—but quite a commonplace, nice boy—made a rather difficult way quite plain to me.

A message ! I will explain.

All my life I have been very much influenced by a Chinese proverb—to the effect that it would be hypocrisy to seek for the person of the Sacred Emperor in a low tea-house. It is a bad proverb, because it is so wise and so enervating. It has " ruined my career."

When, for instance, I founded the *English Review*, losing, for me, immense sums of money on it, or when the contributors unanimously proclaimed that I had not paid them for their contributions—which was not true, because they certainly had between them over £4,800 of Marwood's and my money in their pockets—or when a Suffrage Bill failed to pass in the Commons ; or when some one's really good book has not been well reviewed ; or when I have been robbed, misquoted, slandered or blackmailed, I have always just shrugged my shoulders and murmured that it would be hypocrisy to seek for the person of the Sacred Emperor in a low teashop. That meant that it would be hypocrisy to expect a taste for the Finer Letters in a large public; discernment in critics ; honesty in æsthetes or literati ; public spirit in law-givers ; accuracy in pundits ; gratitude in those one has saved from beggary, and so on.

So, when I first noticed Henri Gaudier—which which was in an underground restaurant, the worst type of thieves' kitchen—those words rose to my lips. I did not, you understand, believe that he could exist and be so wise, so old, so gentle, so humorous, such a genius. I did not really believe that he had shaved, washed, assumed garments that fitted his great personal beauty.

For he had great personal beauty. If you looked at him casually, you imagined that you were looking at one of those dock-rats of the Marseilles quays, who will carry your baggage for you, pimp for you, garotte you and throw your body overboard—but who will do it all with an air, an ease, an exquisiteness of manners ! They have, you see, the traditions and inherited knowledges of such ancient nations in Marseilles—of Etruscans, Phœnicians, Colonial Greeks, Late Romans, Troubadours, Late French—

and that of those who first sang the " Marseillaise " !
And many of them, whilst they are young, have the
amazing beauty that Gaudier had.   Later, absinthe
spoils it—but for the time they are like Arlésiennes.

All those wisdoms, then, looked out of the eyes of
Gaudier—and God only knows to what he threw back
—to Etruscans or Phœnicians, no doubt, certainly
not to the Greeks who colonised Marseilles or the
Late Romans who succeeded them.   He seemed,
then, to have those wisdoms behind his eyes somewhere.   And he had, certainly, an astounding
erudition.

I don't know where he picked it up—but his
conversation was overwhelming — and his little
history of sculpture by itself will give you more
flashes of inspiration than you will ever, otherwise,
gather from the whole of your life.   His sculpture
itself affected men just as he did.   In odd places—
the sitting-rooms of untidy and eccentric poets with
no particular merits—in appalling exhibitions, in
nasty night clubs, in dirty restaurants, one would be
stopped for a moment, in the course of a sentence,
by the glimpse of a brutal chunk of rock that seemed
to have lately fallen unwanted from a slate quarry,
or, in the alternative, by a little piece of marble that
seemed to have the tightened softness of the haunches
of a fawn—of some young creature of the under-
woods, an ancient, shyly-peopled thicket.

The brutalities would be the work of Mr. Epstein
—the others, Gaudier.   For Gaudier's work had just
his own personal, impossible quality.   And one didn't
pay much attention to it simply because one did
not believe in it.   It was too good to be true.
Remembering the extraordinary rush that the season

of 1914 was, it appears a miserable tragedy, but it is not astonishing, that one's subliminal mind should whisper to one, every time one caught that glimpse of a line : " *It is hypocrisy to search for the person of the Sacred Emperor in a low teahouse.*" It was, of course, the Devil who whispered that. So I never got the sensation I might have got from that line. Because one did not believe in that line. One thought : "It is just the angle at which one's chair in the restaurant presents to one an accidental surface of one of these young men's larks."

And then, suddenly, one day, there was no doubt about it. Gaudier was a lance-corporal in the 4th Section, VII Coy., 129th Regt. of Infantry of the Line.* Gaudier was given his three stripes for "gallantry in face of the enemy." One read in a letter :

"I am at rest for three weeks in a village ; that is, I am undergoing a course of study to be promoted officer when necessary during an offensive."

Or in another letter :

"Imagine a dull dawn, two lines of trenches, and, in between, explosion on explosion with clouds of black and yellow smoke, a ceaseless noise from the rifles, a few legs and heads flying, and me standing up among all this like Mephisto—commanding : ' Feu par salve à 250 mètres—joue—feu ! '

"To-day is magnificent, a fresh wind, clear sun, and larks singing cheerfully. . . ."

That was it !
But just because it was so commonplace, so

* The knowledgeable reader will observe that here the writer has consulted the monograph on Gaudier by Mr. Pound—the best piece of craftsmanship that Mr. Pound has put together ; or, at least, the best that this writer has read of that author's.

sordid, so within the scope of all our experiences, powers of observation and recording, it still seemed impossible to believe that in *that* particular low tea-house, there were really Youth, Beauty, Erudition, Fortune, Genius—to believe in the existence of a Gaudier. The Devil still whispered: "That would be hypocrisy!" For if you wouldn't believe that genius could show itself during the season of 1914, how *could* you believe that, of itself, inscrutably, noiselessly, it would go out of our discreditable world, where the literati and the æsthetes were sweating harder than they ever did after *le mot juste*, or the line of beauty, to find excuses that should keep them from the trenches—that, so quietly, the greatest genius of them all would go into that world of misery. For indeed that was a world of misery.

And then I read:

"*Mort pour la Patrie.*

"After ten months of fighting, and two promotions for gallantry on the field, Henri Gaudier-Brzeska, in a charge at Neuville St. Vaast, June 5th, 1915."

Alas! when it was too late I had learned that, to this low teashop that the world is, from time to time the Sacred Emperor may pay visits. For the effect of reading that announcement was to make me remember with extraordinary vividness a whole crowd of drawings, of outlines, of tense and delicate lines that, in the low teahouse of the year before's season, I had just glimpsed at. The Sacred Emperor, then, had been there. He seemed, by then, to be an extraordinarily real figure—as real as Mr. Epstein's brutal chunks of granite.   Only one hadn't seen him because of the crowd.

There are probably several Sacred Emperors still at large, though the best of them will, in duty bound, perhaps have been killed.

IV

I wish I could take for granted the Reader's accept-
ance of the doctrine that Poetry is a matter of the
writer's attitude towards life, and has nothing in the
world to do—nothing whatever in the world to do—
with whether the lines in which this attitude is put
before him be long or short ; rhymed or unrhymed ;
cadenced or interrupted by alliterations or assonances.
One cannot expect to dictate the use of words to a
race ; but it would be of immense service to humanity
if the Anglo-Saxon world could agree that all creative
literature is Poetry ; that prose is a form as well
adapted for the utterance of poetry as verse.   It
would be a good thing, because then Anglo-Saxondom
would come at last into the comity of all other
nations.

In France the novelist or essayist is *Un Poète ;* in
Germany the novelist or essayist is *Ein Dichter ;* in
Italy *Poesia* finds room for all creative writing.   It is
only in Anglo-Saxondom that Poetry is something
silly, impracticable and rhymed, Prose being a thing
which will help you by its commercial instruction to
prosper in your career, to pass examinations, to im-
prove your memory, or increase your salary.   That is
a very lamentable division.

It is a very lamentable division because a race
which, by a mere accident of dialect, arbitrarily walls

off poetry from its intimate life has only a very mediocre chance of conferring upon its component inhabitants even reasonable happiness, and remains a standing menace to the civilisation of its neighbours. That is an aspect of the matter to which we may return. Let us for the moment agree that it is a good thing for men to have, at any rate, some of the comprehension of life that poets have : that it is a bad thing for men to be walled off from the practice of that imaginative sympathy that is the stuff of Poetry.

I will hazard a diagram or so.

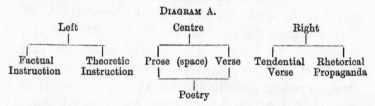

DIAGRAM A.

Left — Centre — Right

Factual Instruction — Theoretic Instruction — Prose (space) Verse — Tendential Verse — Rhetorical Propaganda

Poetry

Or, if you will imagine that you see the above words as representing a political situation, putting it in this way, the image may become clearer :

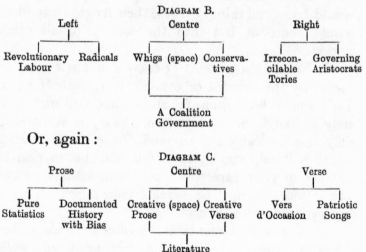

DIAGRAM B.

Left — Centre — Right

Revolutionary Labour — Radicals — Whigs (space) Conservatives — Irreconcilable Tories — Governing Aristocrats

A Coalition Government

Or, again :

DIAGRAM C.

Prose — Centre — Verse

Pure Statistics — Documented History with Bias — Creative (space) Prose — Creative Verse — Vers d'Occasion — Patriotic Songs

Literature

Let me now, taking my courage in my hands and, as it were, creeping about between the mighty legs of the great—and the usually very touchy—ones of the earth, unite these diagrams, and illustrate them with modern instances:

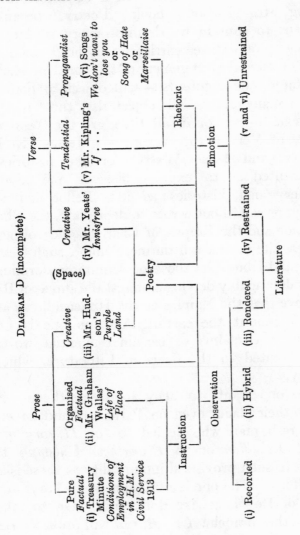

DIAGRAM D (incomplete).

The perspicacious Reader, accustomed to penetrate the wiles of authors, looking at this diagram and perceiving between the divisions of Prose and Verse the word "space," will perceive, here, my little joke . . .

For I will take it that, even if he objects to my calling Mr. Hudson's book "Poetry," because it happens to contain no rhymes—every reader, perspicacious or obtuse, carries in his head some such chart or mental arrangement of the books he reads.

Many—the ergoteurs !—will object to points of detail: many others will object that the truly good books of to-day, or of all time, are the Tendential works of Verse: the verses of Messrs. Kipling, Tupper, and Isaac Watts; or the histories so documented as to express bias of one kind or another—such histories as Mr. Belloc writes to glorify, or as Gibbon wrote to depreciate, the Church of Rome and the Empire of Charlemagne; or, again, to press the matter a little more home, such fruits of tendential labours as those of Mommsen, formidably and indefatigably delving amongst the annals of Rome to prove that the Empire of the Hohenzollerns alone was to inherit the earth. And no one is going to deny the claims of certain tendential work to be accounted to the fields of Literature, which is Poetry.

No one wants to deny to Demosthenes or to Cicero their places even on Parnassus, and he would be a rash man who denied to the *History of the Great Rebellion* or to *Prometheus Unbound* their claims to such provincial immortality as these islands can afford. The one is a monument of Toryism, the other of Revolutionary Radicalism. Or, to take in yet another branch : *Urn Burial* will probably retain its place as a "work of permanent interest," though its writer intended it as at once a work of factual importance and of moral suasion. Yet its "facts" to-day appear absurd and few will be found to be guided by the moral point of view of the author of *Religio Medici*. Nevertheless, few will deny to Clarendon or Browne the names of great prose-writers, or to Shelley that of a great poet. In short, just as politicians of courage and distinction, to remedy particular abuses or at the dictates of conscience, will forsake the benches on which usually they sit and speak in favour of a Government or an Opposition with whom they are normally at bitter variance, so a work of biased documentation may, by reason of the passion or the logical honesty of its author, become a work of great poetry—or a mere patriotic song pass into the undying ranks, amongst the inspired lyrics of the world. It is perhaps just a matter of passion.

Or perhaps it isn't. Let us say that *The Wearing of the Green, Hen wlad fy Nadhau*, and the *Marseillaise* have passed from the classification of merely opportunist patriotism, so that they represent for every soul in the Western world that side of the personality that detests stupid oppression. For we are all— every soul of us—conscious of stupid oppression in this world, whether the oppression be material or spiritual—whether it be applied by dogmatists or freethinkers, by kings or by republics, by great trusts or by leaders of unions. So that that side of the brain desires its cause to be emotionally put. Poetry, on the other hand, would seem to be most surely attained to by practised hands advisedly seeking illustrations of a frame of mind.

" Nine bean rows will I have there, a hive for the honey bee,
  And live alone in the bee-loud glade,
  And I shall have some peace there, . . ."

is at once an expression of a more universal human
aspiration and a more composed piece of selection than
the statements that they are hanging men and women,
or that the day of glory has dawned. So that, on
the whole, we may postulate that a poem written,
with a source of emotion, but with a cool head, has
a greater—an infinitely greater—chance of being
poetry. Nevertheless, in certain white heats of
passion, in certain fanaticisms of propagandists,
immortalities have been achieved, and universal
appeals made. It is possible that white heats of
passion so quicken—or so obscure—men's eyes that
at times they see only the essentials. The statement
that they are killing men and women is a little
matter in the great scale of things—more particularly
for those who have never seen violent death on a
large scale. But the addition " for the wearing of
the green " is an addition of supreme genius, coming
like a flash to an agonised soul. It is thus, if you
are near a sudden death, that you see things.

And the factual-propagandist, or the factual-
biographic, work of prose, even as the propagandist
or tendential piece of verse, may pass over into the
division of literature—by virtue perhaps of its very
inaccuracy. I do not know how high the reader
may be inclined to rate George Borrow. I do not
really know how high I rate him myself; but rate
him high or low, you cannot get away from the
conviction that most of his facts are nonsense,
whether in the *Bible in Spain* or in *Lavengro*—and
that when they are not nonsense they are mendacities.

Yet these very nonsenses and mendacities give to his work such literary quality as it has—for, however they may libel the Man in Black, they make you intimate with the true George Borrow. Similarly with the biographic. Professor Dowden tells us that when Trelawny wrote his *Recollections of the Last Days of Shelley and Byron* he was inspired by a passion for Mary Shelley ; that when, later, he elaborated these into the *Records*, he was inspired by hatred for Mary Shelley, the lady having refused to crown his flame. Professor Dowden tells us that Trelawny was a liar, that speeches he attributes to his subjects, in inverted commas, cannot have been spoken by Shelley, Byron, or Wordsworth. And, indeed, Trelawny was a liar, and the speeches cannot have been delivered just as they are recorded. Nevertheless, the wise man, if he wishes to love Shelley, will read no other record of that frail life— or, indeed, if he wishes to know the true truth about Shelley. For, inspired by passion or by love despised, liar or inventor of unspoken speeches, Trelawny gives us the one—and the very beautiful—picture that humanity will cling to, and in which humanity will believe.

Facts, in short, are all very well. But what is the whole of Mommsen to

" Accedebat huc ebrietas et imprudentia locorum, etiam interdiu obscura. . . ."

And what are all the dreary, dreary labours of Somerset House, the Board of Trade, and the Museum cataloguing staff—all the chatter about Harriet, the analyses of the poet's tradesmen's bills that for ever pour from the press to

"On my coming out, whilst dressing, Shelley said, mournfully,
' Why can't I swim, it seems so very easy ?'
I answered, ' Because you think you can't.   If you determine, you
    will ; take a header off this bank. . . .'
He doffed his jacket and trousers, kicked off his shoes and socks, and
    plunged in, and there he lay, stretched out on the bottom like
    a conger eel, not making the least effort to save himself. . . ."

The lives of poets are dry dust, unless they are
written by poets—as Trelawny was—and poets have
other things to do than to write other poets' lives.
So the terrible half-time civil servants continue to
murder, for us, our only saviours. For, just as
Shakespeare and Jesus were murdered for my friend
Marwood by one set of pedants, so was Shelley
murdered for me by . . . So that I have hardly ever
been able to read a line that came from the pen of
this beautiful spirit.   It is only Trelawny who makes
me love him. . . .

That, indeed, is the function of poetry—to add
to bare, passionate statements the words : " For the
wearing of the green ! " ; or to make us, by a sudden
flash of genius . . . *and there he lay, stretched out on
the bottom, like a conger eel* . . . love our neighbours,
whom the dull procession of the years, the dullness of
our pastors, the dead dullness of our masters, the
dust-dry dullness of those set in literary authority
over us, had rendered distasteful. . . .

I have said enough, I trust, to make it plain to
the most minutely cavilling of readers that, in pro-
pounding my diagrams, I am not trying to impose
any hard and fast—any biologist's—classification. It
is obvious that division shades into division, and that
here is set up the merest wire skeleton, which the
Reader must clothe with his own flesh or sculptor's
wax. As far as I am concerned, the question of
Immortality, of Literary Permanence, of Genius—in

short, of poetry !—this question is simply one of personality.

This statement should, of course, be accepted with some caution and in a reasonable spirit. I do not mean to say that every imaginative writer, as soon as he takes pen in hand, should give himself licence to exaggerate, as Borrow did, his momentary impatience or to avenge his personal dislikes. But I do mean to say that the Public of to-day has to go to imaginative writers for its knowledge of life—for its civilisation.

For this, recorded facts are of no avail.

Facts are of no importance, and dwelling on facts leads at best to death—at worst to barbarism. In the truest sense, it was Mommsen's accumulations that caused what occurred near Gemmenich at six o'clock on the morning of the 4th of August, 1914. . . . But if I, as a Tory, a believer in physical force, an ultimate militarist, am ever forced to throw up my rifle and refuse to fire across a barricade, it will be because Trelawny made Shelley live—and Shelley, a poet whom my early instructors made it impossible for me to read, but a man whom Trelawny made me love, might be on the other side of the barricade !

Expression, then, is the crying need of humanity— and he who sins against any form of expression is . . . Satan. Let us now complete diagram D.

It will have been observed that a space was left in the uncompleted table between Prose and Verse. Here, then, that space is filled in.

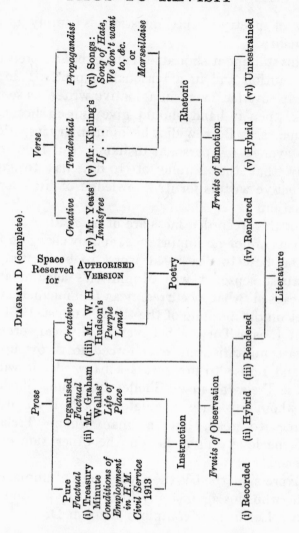

Diagram D (complete).

And so the case for *Vers Libre* is made.

It is made for even the least intelligent reader.
For who in his senses will deny that, between the
entrenched lines of Prosaists and Versificators lies a
No Man's Land that is the territory of Neither-Prose-

Nor-Verse? And few who have given the matter any
attention will deny that this is the oldest, the most
primitive, the least sophisticate form of all literature.
It is the form of incised writing, of marmoreal in-
scription, of the prophets—rhythm !

The Anglo-Parnassian critic of to-day will deny
this, cutting loose from the cyclical tradition that used
to make of these islands one great Bible-reading class.
And the reader who is uninstructed in the literary life
will find this hard to understand. It is not really—
since it is to persons, not principles, that the Anglo-
Parnassian critic objects—Mr. X. hating Mr. Pound
for the love of God ; Mr. Y. Mr. Flint, because
Mr. Flint wishes to find a place for the vastly more
difficult form beside the vastly more easy rhymed
Alexandrines that Mr. Y. can turn out in numbers so
huge. . . .

The other day I wrote to a literary journal to
protest against an editorial in which it had contemptuously dismissed a very beautiful volume of
Vers Libre with the argument that emotion led one
naturally to rhyme. I pointed out that the Book of
Ruth was a work of emotion, and that it contained
no rhyme.

This was, I am nearly sure, the first letter that
ever in my life I had addressed to a public print, and
I watched the resulting controversy with all the
enviable feelings of one undergoing a new experience.
The editorial staff of the paper " squashed " me by
referring me to a passage in which, one hundred years
before, Coleridge had " squashed " Wordsworth. This
passage had nothing to do with the matter, and the
staff ignored the Book of Ruth. A Hebrew gentleman wrote to say that the original Hebrew of Holy

Writ was a metrical performance. But, as I was writing about the English Bible, that forwarded the matter very little. The Hebrew gentleman concluded with contemptuous allusions to my intellect, voice, and personal appearance. A schoolmaster wrote to say that the only true judges of poetry were school children aligned under the pedagogic eye. He stated that he had read poems by myself and Mr. Pound to the children committed to his care by—surely confiding—parents. Only one of my poems had kept those children awake. Therefore I could be no poet. The schoolmaster concluded by proving that I could not be even a person of intelligence because of something or other the *English Review* had done, at a date when the *English Review* had passed to its present editor. The schoolmaster said nothing about the Bible.

A serious student of literature wrote an interesting letter concerning itself with vowel-colourings as they are found in the poets of classical antiquity. The matter was interesting and the letter suggestive —but, again, it contained no reference to the Book of Ruth. The irrepressible Hebrew gentleman, in a further communication, "squashed" the serious student by again alluding contemptuously to my personal appearance and voice. At that happy juncture the editor closed his columns.

I include this account of a quite lively skirmish for several reasons. Firstly: It is important to discover what weapons the Academicists have in their arsenals. (It would at least appear that, from the Courts of Law they have learned that when you have a weak case it is a good thing to abuse the plaintiff's attorney.) And, lastly: (apart from the

fact that a little comic relief may stimulate the reader
to follow me a little further in the consideration of
matters a little more tough : that being a technical
device), I am really interested in the case of the
British Bible.

I may as well say that, since I do not belong to
the Anglican or any other Protestant community, I
am not trying to use any religious weapon against
present-day Academicists. I am talking of the
Jacobean translation merely as a literary achievement.
And it has always appeared to me that most of the
Psalms of David, the Books of Job and of Ruth, and
some of the prophetic writings if, as has been my
good fortune, you can read them with eyes and ears
uncloyed by ecclesiastical chantings and customary
dimnings—just, in fact, as you might read Fitzgerald's
adaptations from the Persian or Mr. Pound's from the
Chinese—these writings, then, in the English language,
as they are printed, and without reference to the
Hebrew original, present an unanswerable case for
rhythmic expression of emotions. I do not say that
they exclude metrical or rhymed expressions, merely
that they present an unanswerable case for the existence of *Vers Libre* as a form.   I do not even mean
to say that the Book of Job justifies the existences of
Mr. Flint, Mr. Pound, H. D., or the French, Italian,
German or North and South American writers of
" free verse "—or even that it justifies the fact that I
am blonde and speak, according to the several gentlemen who have lately addressed the more literary
journals on the subject, with a drawling voice. But
it does give an august precedent for rhythm. . . .

Indeed, the precedent has sometimes seemed to
me to be so overwhelming, the weapon so absolutely

annihilating to opponents that I have hitherto hesitated to use it, as if I had been a commander of a unit who, penetrating immensely far behind enemy lines, meets with no opposition and is afraid of ambushes. And, rack my brains as I will, I cannot think of any enemy reply, unless they will take their courages in their hands and boldly say that the English Bible is rubbish. That is a tenable proposition—but I have not yet come across it in my readings. There are, of course, theological objections to the English Bible, and humanitarians who object to the point of view or proceedings of the prophets. . . .

I suppose I may put myself down as the doyen of living writers of *Vers Libre* in English. Whitman, of course, preceded me in the United States, and W. E. Henley in the United Kingdom, but I cannot think of anyone else, and I can conscientiously aver that neither of these writers had any influence on my own development which I now propose to trace.

This is not vanity. I have already said that I attach little importance to myself as a poet. But I do attach importance to myself as a " specimen," and if I analyse my own progression it is simply because, at a given moment—in 1913–14—I found myself, as a poet, aligned with, and as a critic immensely full of admiration for, a certain group of young men in England and France. And I had been " at it " then for a great number of years already, and I can be more sure of my own development than of that of any of my young friends, so that I can give a better account of it.

And the subject is worth consideration, for, if I can give a proper account of the matter, I ought to be able to lay bare to the reader certain pressures in

the intellectual world.   And, if I could explain those
stresses, I should have gone a long way towards
explaining why the art of literature finds itself to-day
in a position so contemptible, despised and unable to
help itself in the body politic.   For I suppose that
never in a nation fairly self-conscious and sufficiently
open to the influence of poets did Poetry cut less ice
than it does in Anglo-Saxondom to-day.   You might
say that in the eighteenth century there were no poets,
but so avid was the public of poetry that any sort of
metrical, rhymed and printed matter was accepted as
the divine offspring of the Muses . . . To-day !

I think the reader will accept, again, the accuracy
of that constatation.   The causes for it I have dwelt
upon already.   For the moment, let us put it that the
slouch-hatted, bearded, inverness-caped, mouthing—
but extremely slovenly-writing—poets of the 'forties
to 'nineties of the last century had so exceedingly
bored whilst they browbeat the Public, that the
Public had practically finished with Poetry by the
'nineties.   The men of the 'nineties wrote infinitely
better . . . infinitely ! . . . the Dowsons, Johnsons,
Thompsons, Davidsons, and the rest.   Only—*par
pur snobisme !*—they found it as a rule necessary to
indulge in, to promote, vices and bad habits of the
cigarette, Soho-absinthe type.   They revelled pro-
fessionally in squalor.   It was more a matter of the
beau geste than of any real taste or any real necessity.
And it rendered them infinitely provincial—to Soho.

Thus, when the dismal Wilde trial came along,
the Public, still browbeaten by the old guard of those
days but sullenly resentful of earlier, endless, hours
of boredom, simply steam-rollered out, not merely
the prosaists of the Yellow Book, but the entire

singing-bird nest of Vigo Street. Poetry was finished.

For myself I was always so dreadfully afraid of these brilliant ones that they taught me nothing. I had been cowed by the Pre-Raphaelite poets at the age of eight, so effectually that, when at nineteen I published my first novel, I blushed like a youth at his first ball if any one of the brilliant ones hove even distantly in sight. I dare say that saved me from absinthe in Soho.

At any rate, I verily believe that my only real contact with any member of that group occurred at St. James's Hall. That incomparable quartette, Joachim, Piatti, Riess, and Strauss, was fiddling away like mad just under our feet. We were in the shilling seats of the orchestra. Beside me was an eccentric Belgian genius called Knopf, an admirer of my grandfather's; on the other side of him was Verlaine. The quartette finished a movement; Joachim let his fiddle down, moved the handkerchief beneath his chin, and gazed around the hall with that magisterial air of his—and I verily believe he was the most majestic man, for the poise of his head and the glance of his eyes, that I have ever seen. Suddenly, with a bearded filibuster behind him, Mr. Arthur Symons was in front of me, and then sitting beside me. He was proposing that I—and I dare say M. Knopf and Verlaine—should accompany himself and his bearded friend on an expedition into the Spanish Basque Provinces, in order to restore Don Carlos to his throne. I should have liked nothing better. But in those days Mr. Symons was known in my home as the Young Adonis, and I was so shy that I made no answer to the proposal, or possibly a rudely awkward one. The quartette began on its next movement.

I do not know that I have ever again seen or spoken to that great—that marvellously skilful—writer. And if you wish to see what I mean by the good writing of the group that were contemporary with his youth and mine, you have only to consider the work of Mr. Symons, to consider the gap that there would be in a whole genre of English if Mr. Symons had never written. Mr. Symons was undoubtedly the best of his school—his mind was the keenest, his vocabulary the most actual and, in his researches for new rhythmical forms he progressed so far that, possibly, I ought to call him, rather than myself, the doyen of living writers of *Vers Libre*. *At the Stage Door* from *London Nights*, of 1896, is perfect *Vers Libre* according to my own standard. But the actual body of *Vers Libre* by Mr. Symons is relatively small—and I do not know whether, if I made the claim for him, he would be gratified.

And this fact should adumbrate to the reader one of the pressures to which I have referred. I had to make for myself the discovery that verse must be at least as well written as prose if it is to be poetry. Its sentences must be as well constructed ; its thoughts as close ; its language as nervous. The Victorians killed the verse side of poetry because, intent on the contemplation of their own moral importance, they allowed their sentences to become intolerably long, backboneless, and without construction. (They called that poetic licence.) Being too lazy to think out their words, they adopted a sesquipedalian and obsolescent vocabulary, hoping to attract to their verse the glamour of Spenser or Malory. The men

of the 'nineties had " sensed this out." They wrote.
On the whole their sentences, when they wrote in
verse, were as well constructed as prose sentences.
They aimed at a nervous style and a compact form ;
they tried to distil picturesqueness from the life that
was around them.

So that, although their actual leavings are small
and of little attraction to-day, literature, when it
again comes into its own in these islands, will owe
them a great debt of gratitude. Material circumstances drove them out of the world ; but they were
not in any backwater, they were in the main stream
of letters.

For myself, as I have said, I did not learn anything
from them. I wish I had. But I had shynesses and I
had distastes. And, in a sense, I had carried, even then,
my logical progression further than they had carried
theirs. Their ideal of what I will call the surface of
their poems, whether in prose or in verse, was, for me,
too hard and too brilliant. Too self-assertive, and
leaving too much the marks of coruscating chisels !
And I had been too much hammered by the Pre-
Raphaelites. So that my troubled mind took refuge
in an almost passionate desire for self-effacement.
I remember telling Mr. Edward Garnett—or I ought
to put it that my telling Mr. Garnett so shocked him
that twenty years afterwards he recalled the fact to
me—at any rate, I must have told Mr. Garnett in
1893 or so that my one ambition was to pass unnoticed in a crowd. I do not know that my ambition
has ever changed.

But, in those days, that ambition was difficult,
or at least arduous of attainment. If, as a young
littérateur, you desired any of the society at all of

your fellow young littérateurs—and one could not be
human and not desire it!—you had to wear some
parts of a sort of uniform. You might or might
not wear a red tie; might or might not wear a
blue linen, turned-down collar, an inverness, a virgin
beard, a slouch hat. . . . But, if you did not
wear at least one of these regimental badges you
would be ostracised by the intellectuals. I remember
being approached by a formal deputation from a
colony on the outskirts of which I lived. I had had
my slouch hat blown off on Waterloo Bridge, and
had purchased at a Smith's bookstall a cloth cap,
such as golfers wear. The cloth cap, by the colony,
was regarded as anti-social, and I was requested to
scrap it. I could not afford in those days a new
uniform head-covering every other day, and I am
afraid I remained anti-social, and have so remained
to this day.

The incident was symbolic. I resented the
sartorial tyranny, but still more bitterly did I resent
the tyranny of the intellect. It is perfectly true
that humanity divides itself into the stuff to fill
graveyards and the creative artists who carry forward
the work of the world. But it seemed to me then,
as it seems to me now, that it is difficult to be certain
into which division oneself falls. So that no one man
should intellectually browbeat his fellows all the time
—or, indeed, ever, except in moments of heated
personal controversy. And my aspiration to pass
unnoticed in a crowd was intellectual far more than
sartorial. I did not then care how I was dressed,
and I never have cared how I was dressed, except
on parades social or military. But I have always
passionately desired to avoid, either in my person or

my work, anything approaching what it is convenient to call a highbrow attitude.

That appears to me to be plain commonsense for the poet. His poetry must come from his observation of surrounding humanity. If he browbeats his surrounding humanity so that it sits up and, in the effort to live up to its company, behaves pompously, our poet will never see a human being. He will be like a doctor who never sees men's homes at their most sordid, or like a solicitor who is always hampered in court because his clients persist during preliminary consultations in representing themselves as suffering angels.

And even that does not exhaust the disadvantages or exactly make plain my attitude of that day which is my attitude of to-day, though I dare say my attitude of to-day is more benevolent. I mean that if I could get again into those comparatively simple, earnest, and materially self-sacrificing airs of the yet virgin 'nineties, I would very willingly do so, even if it meant wearing a slouch hat, a beard and an inverness! And I should have some peace there. Nevertheless that is a weakness of the flesh and the spirit. And the truth remains that, if we are to get back ever again into the main stream of literature, our attitude must be other. I mean that, just as in our persons we poets must pass in a crowd, so must our verses— our poems. Just as we must sit in bar-parlours and railway offices as the unsuspected great, so must our poems slip into the readings of common men amongst the outpourings of the Yellow Presses and commercial fiction. Only—they must remain in the heart. That is what makes it so difficult.

Yet it is not impossible. I will wager that, if you

chance to read in some vile newspaper, say Mr.
Hudson's story of how the little crow-scaring boy
ran over the immense down, a great way, just to
gaze at the poet passing—I will wager that you will
remember that to the end of your life, long after all
the politics, the controversies, the lusts for blood, the
causes célèbres—all the wilderness of apes a-chatter,
has dried away as the stains of stout dry away from
the mahogany surfaces of public-house bars.   That is
the function of poetry.   But if Mr. Hudson had
written with the tinny self-assertiveness of the Yellow
Book division of the men of the 'nineties he would
have gone, too—he would have gone just as surely
from your mind as has done the incredibly smart drill
sergeant, the descriptive writer of the evening paper,
and innumerable other " characters."   That is the
real proposition.

And that was the proposition that faced me thirty
years or so ago—and I had to face that proposition
in a very deep solitude.   How very deep that solitude
was comes to me in a very clear image.   Mr. Galsworthy had sent me some of his poems in typescript.
And I remember to this day the look of the not very
well typed pages.   Indeed, I remember the poems :

> " The clocks are chiming in my heart
> Their cobweb chime ;
> Old murmurings of days gone by
> The sob of things a-drifting by.
> The clocks are chiming in my heart !
>
> " The stars have flickered and gone out,
> Fair candles blown ! "

And :

> " Straw in the street !
> My heart-strings hearken—
> Fate strums its song of sorrow ! "

And I remember still a great many incomplete

stanzas, though I am sure I have never seen them in print. They gave me a great deal of pleasure. I liked the writer very much. He was writing very charming prose at the time, and I was full of hopes for his literary success. These circumstances made me overcome my natural shyness, and the next time the novelist came to see me I showed him some verses of mine of which I felt rather proud in an unconvinced way. They were called "The Great View," and began :

> "Up here
> Where the air's very clear
> And the hills slope away near down to the bay,
> It is very like heaven. . . ."

It ends :

> "There is France. . . ."

The reader will observe that the poem must have been in rhymed *Vers Libre*, and in an ordinary, non-professional-poetic vernacular. I cannot remember any more of it, and I have not the volume at hand. It must have been written before 1898, but, since no one would print it, it did not, I think, appear until ten years later. Anyhow, it must show that by that date I had pretty well worked out my formula, which was that a poem must be compounded of observation of the everyday life that surrounded us ; that it must be written in exactly the same vocabulary as that which one used for one's prose ; that, if it were to be in verse, it must attack some subject that needed a slightly more marmoreal treatment than is expedient for the paragraph of a novel ; that, if it were to be rhymed, the rhyme must never lead to the introduction of unnecessary thought ; and, lastly, that no exigency of metre must interfere with the personal cadence of the writer's mind or the pressure of the recorded emotion.

The recorded emotion in this particular case was that that I have always felt on seeing France—the most poignant emotion of my life; for when one sees France from the Kentish distance it is as if one saw a freedom, a lightness. . . . But I still remember the puzzled, kindly face of Mr. Galsworthy as he perused those lines. And, after a long pause, he asked why one should be excited at just seeing France. And again: Why were the lines not all of the same length? Poetry was poetry; prose was prose. What was the use of writing poetry if it did not scan? And the point is that I found nothing to answer, because my writing of rhymed *Vers Libre* in those days was purely temperamental. I had no idea of any doctrines; those I have given above I evolved in the succeeding ten or fifteen years. I had felt their presence, and I had just written as I had felt. I have no idea of grumbling at Mr. Galsworthy. He wrote his poetry very beautifully in prose; new departures in verse were no more his affair than they were Flaubert's. And his generosity towards the work of brother artists was always sufficient.

But I think—I am certain—that that was the only one occasion in twenty years in which I even approached a discussion of new verse forms. I do not mean to say that I lacked encouragement. As I have said, the Press always gave me much more space than I could have asked for. Mr. Conrad—as was only proper—was accustomed to inform me almost every day that I was the only English poet that he could even begin to read; and the gentleman who lately wrote to the *English Review* to complain that he had wasted his hospitality on my unworthy self, several times declared—again very properly— that I was the only English poet worth reading. Indeed, I remember one Winchelsea breakfast very clearly.   This gentleman, whilst staying at my house, was making that very agreeable declaration when he stopped in the midst of a eulogistic sentence. His eye had lit upon a packet of patent breakfast food that my household of that day affected.   He grasped the packet, and proceeded to declaim aloud the directions for use printed on it.   And, since this gentleman has, in a printed reminiscence, ascribed to that reading the central idea of one of his most brilliant and entertaining romances, I may well write that breakfast down historic.   And, indeed, the praise I have received, and the encouragement, have always seemed to me to be sufficient.   Only . . . I never had any chance in those days to talk to anyone about the technical side.

I have claimed to be the doyen of living, Anglo-Saxon writers of *Vers Libre ;* and I think that I have established, in my citation of Holy Writ, that *Vers Libre* as a form has a right to exist.   Let me, before returning to my main topic, say a word more as to what it is that does—or should—distinguish the *Vers Libre* of to-day from that of the Elizabethans. Let me invent, for my purposes, the adjective " mouthed."   The Bible, then, and the writings of Whitman have the appearance of poems much more mouthed than, even in the early 'nineties, I could bear.   This is not a derogatory criticism ; certain ages call for more of mouthing than do others, and in its genre the English Bible is perfect and unsurpassable. But that very fact ruled out further excursions into that frame of mind. Whitman made those excursions, so that in his inspiration he was not sufficiently near to the ground ; in his language he was much too much so. Apart from moments of two or three lines, and from one or two longer pieces of sustainedness, his was a vulgarised hybrid language, partly the borrowed phraseology of the Bible, partly the language of American newspaper advertisements. And it was mouthed. At any rate, it was intended to be read mouthingly, with a browbeating scowl at the poor listener.

The same atmosphere hung around Henley. He had an immensely greater verbal skill. Or perhaps that is not generous enough. Let us say that he had a true reverence for words and an almost absolute chastity in the use of them. But his rhythms were almost always ready made. It was less the personal cadence of his mind that he gave us than unrhymed echoes of former metricists. Indeed, it was with Henley when he gave us irregular verse hardly at all a matter of personal cadences ; his irregularities are almost always strings of half- or two-third-finished blank verse lines. As you might say, supposing you to be a musician, they were suspended discords resolving themselves finally into the perfect chord of a blank-line verse :

> " In the waste hour
> Between to-day and yesterday
> We watched, while on my arm—
> Living flesh of her flesh, bone of her bone—
> Dabbled in sweat the sacred head
> Lay uncomplaining, still, contemptuous, strange. "

This is not, of course, the intimate cadence of modern *Vers Libre* ; it is on the marmoreal side of things, tending towards the Elizabethan. But it shows, just as my own verse of the day shows, that this great and upstanding influence on the new day that tried in the 'nineties to dawn had felt the pressure of boredom caused by the loosely written, slowly monotonous, and generally decasyllabic verse of his immediate predecessors. His immediate predecessors would, in fact, have written :

> " In the waste, dragging, stagnant, silent hour
> Between to-day's dawn and dead yesterday
> We watched whilst on my straining, pitiful arm
>
> Dabbled in sweat the sacred, thorn-crowned head."

Henley's verse is a protest against this intolerable tyranny of dullness.

And there were other protests. I suppose that, next to Henley's, the most lasting and devoted influence on the better literature of the last quarter century has been that of Mr. Edward Garnett. And we do not have far to look amongst Mr. Garnett's creative work before we come upon his prose-poems. The Prose-Poem was a form much affected in the early 'nineties. You find it in Fiona Macleod, in the *Black Riders* of Stephen Crane, and in many unexpected places. I dare say that even the Things Seen that Mr. Charles Lewis Hind made fashionable were less consciously rhythmical attempts at finding a short form slightly more memorable and crystallised than ordinary novel, or short story, paragraphs. The Prose-Poem was more elaborated, more self-consciously poetic in atmosphere, more inclined towards fine writing. Nevertheless, I think I shall not be doing Mr. Garnett an injustice if I say that his prose-poems were, too, a Celtic protest against the tautological dullness of his decasyllabic predecessors.

For myself, after a youth rather tortured by the process of being trained for a genius, I was singularly sensitive to these pressures. I will ask the Reader not to believe that I or any of the writers of modern *Vers Libre* are incapable of writing correct verse. Henley undoubtedly could and did. Mr. Pound, as the Reader has seen, formally advises the neophyte to obtain by practice all the metrical and rhyming skill that he can. We are in short inclusive enough. And, for myself, I will cheerfully undertake to write any number of sonnets, Petrarchan or otherwise, at the time-rate of five minutes per sonnet—or two minutes if the rhymes are given. Nay, more, I will undertake to bring at any moment, twenty unselected men from a golf-club or an officers' mess, who, given half a day's tuition, will write sonnets just as fast. The Reader has only to consider how easy fifth-form schoolboys find it to write perfectly correct Latin verse to realise that to write perfectly correct verse in one's own language is so small a feat that it is hardly worth comment. To express an individuality in any medium is another matter; yet that was the quite modest task that I set myself in the early 'nineties. And the task appeared to me to be simply an affair of getting down to one's least rhetorical form of mind, and expressing that. In the end, that seemed to me to be a matter of self-forgetfulness.

The trouble—for me, if not for themselves—with nearly all poets was nearly always that, at any rate, the moment they took pen in hand, they were totally unable to forget that they were professionals, if I may so put it. For myself I simply tried to get at myself in an

absolutely " unpoetic " frame of mind ; I have always
tried to get at that ; I hope so to continue. If I
have any value to the world it is simply the value of
my unaffected self—and I dare say that any man's
value in this world is simply that. For no man's
views are worth very much ; the facts that any man
can collect during his short pilgrimage through life
are ludicrously or pitifully few, and the only empire
over which we can for certain reign, or for which
we can assuredly speak, is the heart of man. And
one's own heart is the heart that one knows best !

I don't mean to say that there is no room in the
world for rhetorical expression ; rhetorical expressions
are, as a rule, the expressions of a man's emotions as
he would like to feel them—or as he would like the
world to believe that he feels them. There is plenty
of room for that, and the room has been well filled.
But of gentle, unaffected, and intimate expression
there has been very little. And the difficulty is simply
that of getting down to oneself—but that is a very
great one. For it is hard for a man to see that the
writing of himself small is his job, and that he must
not swell himself, as if pneumatically, until for a
time at least he shall cast on some stage or other a
shadow as large as that of the Colossus of Rhodes.
Yet, having as a boy seen many such colossi, I had
no other ambition than that of avoiding the colossus
expression. I tried to imagine myself keeping up a
little, intimate warble amongst the hurricanes and
the detonations. I remember writing a poem twenty-
five years ago as a preface to some volume or other.
It was never printed, because Mr. Garnett said it
was not poetry, and I dare say it was not. But it
ended :

"Like poor Dan Robin, thankful for your crumb
Whilst larger birds sing mortal loud, like swearing,
When the wind lulls I try to get a hearing."

And that seems to sum the matter up. Later, I
arrived at the definite theory that what I was trying
to attain to was verse that was like one's intimate
conversation with someone one loved very much. One
would try to render what one was like when, on a
long winter's night before the fire, one talked, and
just talked. No doubt, when one talks to someone
one likes very much, one renders oneself, sometimes,
a shade more virtuous or more picturesque than one
actually is. But then, if the person to whom you are
talking loves you very much, or knows you very
well, they will know you for the odd creature that you
are. And one would be inhuman if one could talk of
oneself as dispassionately as, let us say, an editor of
the *New Statesman*.

Having then, as it were established the tone, let
us go on to the question of cadence for intimate
verse. . . . We are attempting to establish some sort
of formula for the revelation of intimacies; for the
revelation, the rendering, not the recording. What,
then, is the most intimate, the most revelatory attribute
of the men with whom we do our daily businesses?
Supposing you, a short, stout man, desire to personate
for the amusement of your friends a tall, thin lady,
how do you set about it? You imitate the tones of
her voice if you can get your voice anywhere near
hers. If you cannot, you reproduce her vocabulary,
the turns of phrase that she most characteristically
uses—and the cadence of her sentences.

The writer of intimate verse cannot render tones
of voice, the rest he can and must. That is to say

that, supposing the poet accepts as his my ambition, and desires that his verse shall exhibit him as he really is, whether he be merely talking to a friend, flying in an aeroplane, or indulging in any intermediary activities—the poet then must seek to reproduce his actual vocabulary, his own characteristic turns of phrase, the exact cadence of his own usual sentences. The result will be himself.

That will be no easy task. Let the Unpractised Reader try to write merely a short note to a tradesman, and he will find that the phraseology he employs is that of dead and gone generations of notewriters. Let him go a little further, and try to write an exposition of some moral truth, or an account of some mental adventure, and he will find, after he has written it, that he has employed phrases from Addison's *Spectator*, cadences from Doctor Johnson's *Lives of the Poets*, and the vocabulary, again let us say, of one of the editors of almost any dignified journal of to-day. There will be nothing of the writer's self.

That, then, is the case of *Vers Libre* as it has presented itself to me during a matter of thirty years. I may as well add a note or two as to rhyme. I have personally used rhyme very frequently, firstly because I like rhyme and vowel colourings in verse, and secondly because rhyme appears to have the effect of hastening verse along. I once wrote an immensely long poem in unrhymed Vers Libre—and it seemed immensely long and immensely wearisome ! It was called *On Heaven*. I went through it again a month or so later and added rhymes to a great many lines. It at once seemed shorter and less wearisome. I fancy that the reason for this is that the mind, looking out for rhymes, hastens the tempo of its reading in order to achieve satisfaction. For the same reason I avoid and rather dislike alliteration : the reading mouth seems to slow down in order to prepare for the impinging of the consonants. . . .

But I don't condemn even assonances : you may have reasons for slowing your verse down—and I think that both Mr. Pound and Mr. Flint uphold them ; but then they have not been so trained in the harder and more chaste school of prose. But indeed I condemn nothing that will give you pleasure and make for fun—or I should not admire, as I have said I do, the work of Mr. Huxley and Miss Sitwell.

I do not even wholly condemn obvious displays of personal cleverness. A high-spirited young thing juggling with phrases as a juggler juggles with plates is a delightful spectacle—only one has to remember that, in the end, Art is more mighty than any one's self. In the end one should remember that the expression of one's true self is the work in hand—not the gaining of plaudits because in lovely tights and never so bright spangles, in the intoxicating limelight, one throws thirteen gilt balls a hundred times towards the intoxicated moon !

You will remember that Dr. Johnson at Vauxhall or some such place said that the spectacle of that illuminated and joyous multitude made him feel profoundly melancholy. He could not but remember that each of those individuals had awaiting him or her a fireside where solitude and misgivings are the portion of humanity. . . .

It is the province of Literature to await those returning revellers, to give them courage, and to accompany them through their solitude.

V

SECOND CODA

I

FEROCITY, then, is not the note of this Message to an Uninstructed but Intelligent Reader. . . . I may, I mean, have used here and there a sentence that will shock; but that is not because I am unacquainted with refinement. I may have used here and there a phrase expressive of contempt: but I am not really, nor do I seek to make the Reader, exclusive. Let us be omnivorous—for that you have the example of Mr. Conrad; let us be admiring; inclusive; generous. . . . But let us know where we are going.

For myself, indeed, I am so soft hearted that I could not bear to cut the throat even of the Typical Critic, the parasite on the late George Crumb. I would not abolish his *Literary Journal*, deprive him of his war-profits and positions or his ascendancy in parlours and parlour games. He would like to abolish me and, when this book falls under his reviewing hands, will seek to do so, just as, in 1916, he declared officially that I had died—of drink, I believe. That is all in the commercial side of the game. . . .

No, accretiveness is an innocent trait in human nature, whether you establish a corner in the topography of George Crumb or amass an infinite number of instances of the use of the word "until" by Bunyan. (He might have written "till" and ingenious race theories have been built up—in, let us say, Tuebingen on these tabulations.)   But these things have nothing to do with Literature.   They supply a craving for mental anodynes, much as gin will do. They are, of course, more suited to the drawing-rooms of the non-productive classes.   They are the dominant preoccupation of the Intelligentsia, and there the matter ends.

Or perhaps it does not.   Perhaps the matter needs more words.   I may seem to have been too contemptuous of printed matter.   I read this morning in the *Manchester Guardian* a pious aspiration that in England in 1921 the number of factual books published may prove to exceed that of works of the imagination—and I sit and wonder at this acharnement at this date.   Heaven knows I do not despise the literary achievements of scientists or of Men of Action, nor do I in the least desire to limit their activities.   But I fail to see why the political leaders of the world should plump so violently for the educative value of, let us say, manuals on reinforced concrete—for the works that shall make us more materialist or more efficiently acquisitive.   The function of our political-educative masters is primarily —and to-day more than ever—to teach us how to live together in concord and decency.   Then, to put efficiency in acquisition before civilisation is to put a violent explosive into a very shaky cart on a rough road. In the vulgar phrase it is asking for trouble. . . .

Still, if people want trouble, I do not see why they should not have it.

Nevertheless, the way towards civilisation, is probably through the Schoolroom.   As I have already said, the most factually-gifted soul that I

have met in my career through the world was that of
Arthur Pearson Marwood, the North Yorkshire—
nearly Durham—squire's son who shared with myself
the expenses and the odium of the *English Review*.
Temperamentally, like all Tories and most Englishmen, he was a poet. That is shown by the share he
had in that periodical. . . . Owing to Education, like
nearly all Englishmen and most Tories, he had a
stout, but penetrable, super-surface of defiant, but
sometimes shamefaced Materialism. He was a Senior
Wrangler ; had an extraordinary knowledge of the
pedigrees and public form of racehorses, and had
evolved a really infallible System for defeating the
tables at Monaco. I have tried it many times and
always with success—but it worked so slowly and
needed such patience in the carrying out that I have
never risen from the tables a winner, since I always
threw away an evening's winnings and a good deal
more on a last, sheer gambling, chance.

I once discussed for a whole evening with him the
characters of Shakespeare and of Our Redeemer.
He said they both bored him—and he was perfectly
serious. He got eventually out of the discussion by
saying that both Shakespeare and Christ had for him
the aspects of Modern Educators. Firstly, he had
seen them as if with the features of the " English "
master of Clifton, and then with the spectacles
and uncombed beards of Professors Schlegel, Tieck,
Hauffmann and Winterhausen, the commentators of
the text of Shakespeare ; or with the features—whatever the features were—of Strauss who wrote the
Leben Jesu and of Dean Farrar who, in collaboration
with that most delightful and humorous of pedants,
Dr. Richard Garnett, wrote the *Life of Christ*.

And it seemed such a tragic thing that the beautiful spirit of Arthur Marwood should have the beautiful features of Shakespeare and of Our Lord ruined for him by one English schoolmaster and by innumerably pullulating professors that . . . I will not complete the sentence. . . . Or let me put it that many—a great many—of us have seen certain landscapes and certain cities with certain familiar adornments. A great many—a great, great many—never saw any landscapes more. They were avenging for the awful and wronged shade of my friend Marwood, the be-schoolmastered and be-professored visages of the man who wrote *Lear* and the Man who died on the Tree.

For if you turn Shakespeare and Christ into schoolmasters and professors there will remain nothing for you but Armageddon.

II

And, what made it all the more unbearable was that the master at Clifton (which is, I believe, in a suburb of Bristol) who taught Marwood to be bored— but . . . bored to distraction!—by *Lear* and the Parables was T. E. Brown, a very beautiful poet who hated his job. He was forced by the System to corrupt young minds and so he made his bread and kept his family in respectable circumstances, whilst corresponding with W. E. Henley from the reputable suburb of Bristol and the Suspension Bridge!

There is something very symbolic about all this. . . . Clifton is memorable because of its Suspension Bridge, one of those silly toys that were the wonder of the world, Victoria Albertoque regentibus. It is

detestable because there, in Clifton School, two fine
minds were martyrised so that the world might come
into the mould of Victoria and of Albert. . . .

Two fine minds were, then, ruined by Clifton—
those of a beautiful poet and of a Yorkshire squire who
might well have saved the world by Toryism. (For
I take it, not being anything but a fanciful politician,
that the world might be saved by Toryism, just as well
as by Bolshevism, which is probably the same thing.
. . . And I should like to say very quickly that I am
imputing nothing against the fine, conscientious men
who made Clifton School what it is, or against the
pupils that it has turned out. . . . For it is certainly
saying nothing against Arthur Marwood to say that
he was rendered tuberculous by the fact that Clifton
was a "cramming" school; and it is saying nothing
against T. E. Brown to say that loyally he enforced
the Battalion Orders of the Force in which he had
enlisted. . . . I am saying merely that the Unit
itself was damnable.)

You may take a further analogy from the poor
dear old ex-Service men whom to-day we are all
engaged in boycotting. If you watch some miserable
tramp regarding the Guards doing squad drill with
or without arms on the Square, you will observe a
certain connoisseurship in the tramp's eyes. He will
be able to tell you which is the smartest, which is
the awkward, squad, and he will be keen upon the
differences. . . . That is because, to his undoing, he
was once taught that technique; he too, once,
upon the word three, cut the right hand smartly
away to the side. . . . And there are mornamillion
of us tramps; enough to make connoisseurship in
drill almost a folk-knowledge. . . .

The poetic analogy is almost exact. If we had had no public Education we might or might not have retained forms of popular art. But we have popular education, and it has certainly killed popular art. . . . It sounds like democratic cant to say that you can have no art in a nation if you have no popular art : it is none the less a profound truth. We have not the great poets of Athens because we have not the popular appreciation and because our populace have not the knowledge.

The ana that our "English" Masters, our University Professors, and our Typical Critics, force upon our children, our undergraduates, and our adults, have killed the taste, have engendered a nearly vomiting distaste, for Poetry in these nations. . . . What, then, is the remedy ? . . . It is simply to pension off all these perfectly honourable, high-minded, and above all industrious gentlemen, who are themselves the victims of the System. Pension them off and, whilst the State has that burden upon it, simply turn your children and your undergraduates loose for so many hours a week, in libraries and let them alone. As the pensions fall vacant you might appoint other gentlemen to give lessons in prosody —lessons on the Sonnet, the Triolet, on rhymed Iambics, on blank Verse. But this would be merely squad drill with arms — an absolute national necessity, having the same relationship to Poetry that our evolutions on the square at Chelsea Barracks had to the later assaults upon the Enemy lines. For, as long as the knowledges thus imparted were perfectly definite and technical they would be very useful : but all attempts at dogmatising about taste by these Professors should be treated as penal offences.

Children should then be forced to write sonnets, triolets, rhymed Iambics, and they should be smacked if they took words out of books; undergraduates should be gated for the same offence. . . .

In a very few years you would have a nation, not only of heroes: you would have a nation back at at least the musical standard of England in pre-Hanoverian days, and a nation, not of verse-writers, but of individuals fairly competent to observe, upon the drill-grounds, the evolutions of the Poets. For—as you may read in Pepys—in the barbers' shops, Charles II being king, there were laid out the instruments of a quartette party. One gentleman, waiting for a shave, would pick out a "ground" on a viol da gamba, and the remaining customers would improvise parts above that ground. His shaving finished, the gentleman in the chair would stay to complete the Consort, rather than, hastening away, to gain fourpence on 'Change. . . . For myself I hope, yet, to compete for a prize in sonnets written *bouts rhimés* whilst a waiting barber—deferential out of respect for the Muse—fidgets a little and whispers: "Your turn next, sir."

That may seem over-sanguine. And yet, it may not be. We may read almost every day in the organs of the Intelligentsia that the day of the Intelligentsia, all Europe through, is done. It is the one thing needed to save us from barbarism.

For the moment the vested interests, the whole forces of Commercialism are apparently impenetrable. The reader must remember that gentlemen have spent millions of pounds and years of labour in conquering distastes for the duller passages of Goethe, Milton, or the more uninspired mediæval

Romances; in acquiring exact knowledges of typographical errors in folios and the love-letters of poets. These gentlemen will not willingly let those sums and those hours be called wasted. The Periodical Press has had untold millions of pounds invested in it. It will not willingly let a taste for more permanent letters filter through to a public that would then appraise more justly the periodical press. This is probably an unconscious pressure. Or, again, you have the vested interests of publishers with more millions invested in dull and incapable Classics. This may seem a trifling thing—and indeed it is a minor obstacle. I saw the other day a letter from a very old firm of publishers to a writer who, in a preface had said something contemptuous about the compiler of an Anthology of the 'Sixties. They had commissioned the new preface — it was not for that particular Anthology—and they wrote seriously and with pain. They asked the writer how he could expect them to publish his sneer. They had thousands of pounds invested in plates for the Anthology; they made a yearly profit of several thousand pounds from this investment. And they had duties to their shareholders.

It was a very reasonable letter. I myself once had a preface "turned down" by a reputable firm. I had written it for nothing to oblige some one. In the course of it I had occasion to praise highly the work of a writer who was published by another firm. The active partner of this firm told me—with a great deal of fury—that I must be a fool if I thought he was going to help praise the wares of a brother tradesman!

I do not blame either firm over much: they each

had shareholders, creditors, employees, establishments. . . . And I suppose men must live!

But the Reader should remember that these
things do exist, and do form a very solid barrier
against the progress of human thought and of human
inter-expression. So the Reader should do what he
can—all that he can!—to help young, new writers
who do not have a very good time. And some old
ones too!

I used to love a sonnet of Wordsworth's. It was,
I think, an introductory poem to a first edition of
the *Excursion* that I possessed as a boy. Some one
stole the book from me long ago, and, look as I
may through collected editions of Wordsworth, I
have never been able to find it again. It began:

"The stars that from the zenith pour their beams,"

and went on, I think,

"Visible though they be to half the world,
Though half a world be conscious of their brightness. . . ."

But in that case it cannot have been a sonnet.
I have not seen it for thirty years. . . .

At any rate, in the course of a rather troublesome
life, I have usually been upborne by the remembrance
of the last two lines of this poem. In case—for one
never knows—I should henceforth be censored out
of existence by my young Parnassian friend, muzzled
by publishers, or truly die of drink and so never
write a word more, I here present those two last
lines to young writers as a gift, a testament, a
consolation, a buckler. They are:

"So, to the measure of the light vouchsafed,
Shine, poet, in thy place and be content!"

INDEX

A

Academe, 20, 22
Academicians, 13; their slumbers, how disturbed, 64
Academicism, 12, 15; its triumph (1921), 61, 63, 135, 136
Academicists, treatment for, 21; their cheques, 25; their weapons, 106–8
Addison, J., 104, 214
——, *Spectator*, 16, 214
Aeschylus, 22
Albert, 77, 108
Albert, Prince Consort, 219–220
Aldington, R., 59, 64, 67, 136
American Journal, A serious, 25
Ammianus Marcellinus, his home life, 59
Andersen, Hans, 133
Argentine Republic, 74
Aristophanes, Frere's translation of *Frogs* quoted, 127, 144, 150, 162
Army Council Instructions, 9
Artaxerxes, 15
Athens, 62
Atlantic Monthly, its correspondents, 28
Authorised Version (of Holy Writ), 36, 69, 85, 152, 194 8, 208

B

Bauch, Professor, 4
Baudelaire, C., 104
Beardsley, A., 38
Bécourt, Bois de, 79, 108
Beddoes, T. L., 152
Belgium, Invasion of (1914), 60
Belloc, H., 188

Bennett, E. Arnold, 26, 30–31, 45, 56, 58
——, *Truth About an Author, The,* 30
——, *Man From the North*, 31
Bible, English. See *Authorised Version*
Blast, 140
Born, Bertran de, 167–8
Borrow, G., 190–1, 193
——, *Bible in Spain*, 190
——, *Lavengro*, 190
Boston, Mass., 28, 104
Braddon, Miss M. E., 53
Brawne, Fanny, 141
Brede Place, 111–13, 122
Bridges, Robert, Poet Laureate, 26, 56, 130, 155
Brown, Ford Madox, 174, 175, 176
Brown, T. E., 219–220
Browne, Sir T., 36, 39, 74
——, *Religio Medici*, 189
——, *Urn Burial*, 74, 188
Browning, R., 130, 131, 133, 152, 153–4, 162
——, *Flight of the Duchess*, 131
——, *Red Cotton Nightcap Country*, 154
Brzeska. See Gaudier, H.
Burlington House, Immortals of, 61
Byron, Lord, 9, 164, 191

C

Cabaret Club, 141
Cambridge, Mass., 29
Cannae, 65
Catullus, 22, 154
Censorship, Neo-Academic, 62, 64
Cervantes, 16

Chamberlain, Rt. Hon. J., his hidden aims, 59
Charlemagne, 188
Charles II. (of England, etc.), 222
Chateaubriand, F. A., 17
Chaucer, G., 16
Chelsea Barracks, 220–1
Chevy Chace, 162, 165
Chesterton, G. K., 154
——, *Robert Browning*, Monograph, 154
Churchill, J. *See* Marlborough
Cicero, T., 188
Clarendon, Edward Hyde, Earl of, 188
——, *History of the Great Rebellion*, 187
Coleridge, S. T., 147
Colvin, Sir S., 39, 195
Concord Group, 28
Conrad, Joseph, 18, 26–7, 99, 34–5, 39–41, 44, 46, 51–4, 69–70 ; and Anglo-Saxondom, 79–101, 105, 119, 140, 207, 216
——, *Almayer's Folly*, 72, 80, 97
——, *Chance*, 79–81, 87
——, *Falk*, 98
——, *Heart of Darkness*, 34, 72, 90, 97, 98
——, *Lord Jim*, 34, 72, 86, 88–90
——, *Nigger of the Narcissus*, 41, 81
——, *Nostromo*, 90, 91
——, *Secret Agent*, 91–3
——, *Outpost of Progress*, 91
——, *Smile of Fortune*, 97–8, 101
——, *Typhoon*, 108
——, *Under Western Eyes*, 87, 91, 99
——, *Youth*, 34, 72
—— with F. M. Hueffer : *Inheritors*, 35 ; *Romance*, 35, 70, 71, 114
" Conway " (Training Ship), 89
Cooper, F., 85, 86
——, *Two Admirals*, 86
Courbet, G., 138, 174
Covent Garden Market, its neighbourhood, Parnassian, 25
Crackanthorpe, H., 37, 38
Crane, Stephen, 17, 39, 69, 73, 75 ; and the Mainstream, 102–112, 115, 119, 120, 211
——, *Black Riders*, 110
——, *Bride Comes to Yellow Sky*, 108

Crane, Stephen, *Maggie, A Child of the Streets*, 108
——, *Open Boat* (quoted), 39
——, *Red Badge of Courage*, 106, 108
——, *Three White Mice*, 108
——, *Third Violet*, 108
Crébillon, P. J. de, 104, 159
Critics (of the Periodical Press). *See* Reviewers.
Critics, Typical English, their necrological activities, 11 ; their good fellowship, 12 ; described, 169–172, 216
Crumb, George (Imaginary Poet), his biography, 11 ; his Minor Works and Love Letters collected, 170, 216
Cubists, 25, 60, 62, 137–140, 149, 174
Cummings, Mr., 54–5

D

Daily Telegraph, a review quoted from, 50
Dane, Miss Clemence, 65
Daniel, Arnaut, 166
Dante, 21, 69
Darcy, Ella, 37
Darley, G., 152
Dartmoor, 67
Daudet, A., 80
Dee, Dr. (Alchemist), 74
Defoe, Daniel, 16, 17, 104
De la Mare, W., 130, 155
Demosthenes, 188
Dial, 122
Dickens, C., 13, 42, 174
——, *Little Dorrit*, 42
Diderot, D., 16–17
——, *Neveu de Rameau*, 16
Divorce Court, disliked by readers, 83–4
Doolittle, Miss H. *See* H. D.
Doughty, C. M., 26, 56
Douglas, Norman, 59, 136
Dowden, Professor E., 39, 191
Dowson, E., 199
Dryden, J., 152
Dunsany, Lord, 26, 56

E

Earth's Greatest Writer, 21, 22.
 See also Novelist, Eminent
Edinburgh Review, 134
Elgin Marbles, 177
Eliot, T. S., 26, 56, 64, 104
Embryology, Societies of, their
 chronicles, Literature, 5
Emerson, R. W., 28, 102, 146
Eminent, The, their character-
 istics, 21; list of, 26, 57; disin-
 clined for cohesion, 58
Eminent Novelist. See Novelist,
 Eminent
Encyclopædia Britannica, 146
"English" Masters, 12, 219
English Review, 8, 58–60, 122, 136,
 179, 196, 207
Epstein, J., 136, 140, 175, 181, 183
——, Rock Drill, 140
Erasmus, D., 166
Euripides, 16, 127

F

Fabian Society, 169
Farrar, Dean R., 218
——, Life of Christ, 218
Fielding, Henry, 42
Fine Writing, Directions for, 52
Flaubert, G., 9, 22, 39, 42, 57, 81,
 88, 93, 105, 110, 114–5, 159–161
——, Cœur Simple, 138
——, Correspondence, 115
——, Education Sentimentale, 159
——, Madame Bovary, 160
——, Trois Contes, 159–60
Flint, F. S., 23, 59, 64, 67, 149,
 (quoted) 158, 159, 160, 166, 167;
 death announced, 171, 173, 194–7
——, Otherworld, (quoted) 23, 160
Ford, H., 100
Forman, Buxton, 141
Fort, P., 171
France, A., 100, 166
——, Crime de Silvestre Bonnart,
 166
Frederick, H., 38
Frere, J. Hookham, Translations of
 Aristophanes quoted, 127; Re-
 view of Mitchell's Translation,
 144
Futurists, 25, 40, 60; a byword, 61

G

Galsworthy, J., 31, 84, 205, 207;
 Poems quoted, 205
——, Villa Rubein, 31
Garnett, Edward, 38, 39, 65, 106,
 107, 110, 202, 210, 212
——, An Imaged World, 210
Garnett, Dr. R., 218
Gaudier-Brzeska, Henri, 136, 171,
 173–84
Gaudier, Joseph, 179
Gemmenich, 193
"George Egerton," 37
Giffard, S., 172
Gissing, G., 38
Goncourt, Brothers, 57
Gosse, Edmund, 26, 56
Graham, R. B. Cunninghame, 29,
 75
Grimm's Fairy Tales, 133
Guzman D'Alfarache, 15

H

"H. D." (Miss Doolittle), 59, 64,
 104, 136, (quoted) 157, 159, 162,
 163, 166, 171, 197
Hardy, Thomas, 26, 27, 34, 39, 56,
 58; his poetical methods, 153–5,
 164, 165
——, Sunday Morning Tragedy, 58,
 165
Harris, Frank, 38
Harland, Henry, 36–8
Hauch, Professor, 4
Hauffmann, Professor, 218
Hawthorne, Nathaniel, 28
Hazlitt, W., 13
Hecuba, 33
Heine, Heinrich, 133, 165
Henley, W. E., 17–18, 27–28, 31, 35,
 57, 66, 198, 209, (quoted) 209–
 10, 219
"Henrietta Maria," 18, 111, 121
Hen Wlad fy Nadhau, 189
Hogarth, W., 174
Hohenzollerns, 188
Holmes, O. W., 28, 104
Homer, 13, 15, 21, 32–3, 162
——, Odyssey, 33
Howells, W. D., 104, 105

Hudson, Henry (The Navigator), 74
Hudson, W. H., 26, 27, 29, 52, 56, 58; and the simple word, 68–78, 187, 194, 205
——, *Birds in a Village*, 70
——, *Green Mansions*, 69, 70
——, *Hampshire Days*, 70
——, *Nature in Downland*, 70, 77
——, *Purple Land*, 70, 187
——, *Shepherd's Life*, 70, 76
Hueffer, F. M. *See* Conrad, J.
Hugo, V., 160, 171
Hunt, W. Holman, 45
Hunt, J. H. Leigh, 172
Huxley, Aldous, 144, 215

I

Imagistes, 25, 40, 60, 62, 137–140, 149, 161, 174
Imagistes (Anthology), quoted 157–8
Immortals. *See* Academicists
Impressionism, 25, 60, 61, 62; its canons, 138–9
Inn of Letters, its Coffee and Commercial Room, 12
Irving, Sir H., 19
Irving, Washington, 28

J

James, Henry, damned by Eminent Novelist, 8; birthplaces of, imaginary, 29, 35, 36, 37, 39, 40, 41–2, 46–9; his views of Marlow, 53–4, 56, 58, 100, 101; and the Mainstream, 102–125
——, *Altar of the Dead*, 49
——, *American*, 36
——, *Daisy Miller*, 28, 36, 113
——, *Death of the Lion*, 34
——, *Europe*, 103
——, *Four Meetings*, 103
——, *Great Good Place*, 34, 49, 121
——, *Passionate Pilgrim*, 103
——, *Princess Casamassima*, 36, 42
——, *Real Thing*, 34, 41, 117
——, *Sacred Fount*, 49
——, *What Maisie Knew*, 34, 108
——, *Wings of the Dove*, 123

Jeunes, Les (of 1914), 26, 59, 60, 62, 64, 135
Joachim, J., 200
Job, Book of, 197
Johnson, Lionel, 199
Johnson, Dr. Samuel, 28, 214, 215
——, *Lives of the Poets*, 214
Jonson, Ben, 28, 163
Joyce, J., 64–5

K

Keats, J., 141, 142, 147, 148, 152, 164, 172
——, *Eve of St. Agnes*, 147
——, *Last Sonnet*, 148
Kieff, Government of, its bourgeoises, 7, 29
King's Road, Chelsea, 4
Kipling, Rudyard, 26, 38, 56, 157, 185
Knopf, W., 200
Kurzeniowski, J. C. *See* Conrad, J.
Kyd, F., 100

L

Lafarge, Mrs. H., 117
Lamartine, A. M. L. de P., 171
Lamb, C., 13, 51, 75
La Plata, 29
Lawrence, D. H., 26, 56, 59, 64, 136
Legallienne, R., 110
Legenda Aurea, 166
Lily, J., 28, 147
——, *Euphues*, 147
Literary Artists, their proscription, 57, *et passim*
Literary Journal (Imaginary Periodical), account of fracas between Mr. P. and Lawrence Queue, 4–5, 15, 20, 141, 142, 170–1, 216
Littérateur of England, his stimuli, 57

M

Macchiavelli, N., Letter to Francesco Vittori, 1
Macleod, Fiona, 210

Mainstream of Literature, 16–18 ; Henry James, Stephen Crane, and the, 102–125
Malaysia, 93
Malbrouk. *See* Marlborough
Malory, Sir T., 147, 201
——, *Morte D'Arthur*, 74, 147
Manchester Guardian, 217
Margaret of Navarre, 43
Marinetti, A., 140
Marivaux, P. C. de C. de, 17, 104
——, *Marianne*, 16
" Mark Rutherford," 38
Marlborough, John Churchill, first Duke of, 5-6
Marlow, Christopher, 100, 147
Marlow (Conrad character), 34, 53-4, 95
Marryat, Captain, 85, 86
——, *Percival Keene*, 86
Marseillaise, 189, 190
Marwood, A. P., 58–60, 136, 180, 218–220
Masters, E. Lee, 136
Maupassant, Guy de, 15, 57, 104, 110, 114–15, 138, 159–161
——, *Fort Comme la Mort*, 97
——, *Maison Tellier*, 86
Maximilian, 47
Mayne, Miss E. C., 36-7, 66
——, *Blind Man*, 36
Meggott, Miss Annie, 54
Meredith, G., 34, 39, 56, 58, 59
——, *Emilia*, 42
——, *Evan Harrington*, 34, 41
Meynell, Mrs. W., 26, 56
Millais, Sir J. E., 175
Milton, J., 22
Minerva, 61
Mommsen, T., 188, 191, 193
Monro, H., 58, 156
——, *Some Contemporary Poets*, 156
Montaigne, imitated by Mr. Peskith, 69, 74
Montana, University of, its Laundry Bills, 5
Moore, George, 26, 32, 34, 45, 56, 105, 159
——, *Ave Atque Vale*, 32
Morning Post, 159
Mots Justes, formula for, 51-5
Musset, A. de, 17, 150
Mystères de Paris, 86

N

Neuville St. Vaast, 177, 183
Newbolt, Sir H., 26, 56
New England, 70, 74, 103, 104, 116
Newport, R. I., 29
New Statesman, 213
Novel, the, its Form, 42-6
Novelist, Eminent ; his letter to the *English Review*, 8, 21; his technical maxim, 29 ; quoted as to methods of composition, 29–30, note ; recommends *Man from the North*, 31; the writer lectures him on the Sonata form, 45–46, 207–8
——, Enormously Popular, his " technique," 81-4, 94

P

P., Mr., 4-5
Pain, Barry, 38
Parnassus (England's-), 26, 57, 60, 61, 65
Pater, Walter, 59
Pepys, S., 222
Peskith, Mr. (Imaginary Author). *See* Montaigne
Petrarch, 13
Petronius, 22, 191
——, *Satyrikon* (quoted), 101
Philadelphia, Pa., 28
Philaster (quoted), 101
Pinker, J. B., 109
Podmore's Brother, 138
Poe, E. A., 32–3, 104–5
——, *Gold Bug*, 33
——, *Pit and the Pendulum*, 33
Poet of the Pole Star, 151
Poetry, Professors of, 6, 221
Poland, 87, 93, 100
Pole Star, Hymn to, its composition, 145-7
Pope, A., 13, 21, 152, 164
——, *Dunciad*, 21
Pound, E., lectures the Writer, 45, 59; his decease, 61-2, 104, 131, 136 ; a walk with, 139–140, 143 ; his re-visitation, 143–4, 149 ; quoted, 158, 159, 163, 166, 167-8, 169, 170, 171 ; his further decease, 171, 173, 194, 195, 196, 197, 211, 215

Pound, E., *Gaudier Brzeska*, a monograph, 182
——, *Goodly Fere*, 170
——, *Pavanes and Divisions* (quoted), 142
Pre-Raphaelite Brotherhood, 57, 81, 202
Psalms of David, 197
Pseudonym Library, 38

Q

Quarterly Review, 134, 150, 172
Queue, Lawrence, 4, 15

R

Rabelais, 69, 74
Railway Guide (*Bradshaw*), 79, 84
Rapin, R. P., 104
Read, H., 67
Regnier, H. de, 171
Rembrandt van Rhyn, 174
Reviewers, their paucity of epithet, 21, 63. *See also* Critics
Richardson, Miss Dorothy, 64–5
Richardson, S., 16–17, 104
——, *Clarissa Harlowe*, 16–17
——, *Pamela*, 16
Rodin, A., 174
Romantic Movement, French, 181
Ronsard, 150
Rossetti, Christina G., 130, 131, 132, 154
——, D. G., 110, 147, 148, 152
——, W. M., 39
Rousseau, J. J., 16
Ruth, Book of, 195, 196, 197
Rye, 39, 46–9, 113, 114, 115, 123, 124

S

Sainte-Beuve, G., 171
Sand, Georges, 125
——, *Consuelo*, 81
Sappho, 146, 147
Sartor Resartus, 86
Scheherezade, 44
Schnitzler, A., 160
Scott, Sir W., 13

Self - Inflicted Wounds. *See* Wounds, Self-Inflicted
Shakespeare, W., 13, 22; as novelist, 42–3, 51, 69, 152, 156, 163, 218, 220
——, *Hamlet*, 19
——, *King Lear*, 42
——, *Tempest*, 101
Shelley, Harriet, 19
Shelley, Mary, 191
Shelley, P. B., 121, 141, 148, 152, 191–2, 193
——, *Hymn to Pan*, 147
——, *Prometheus Unbound*, 18
——, *To Sleep*, 147
Sinclair, Miss May, 26, 56, 66
Sitwell, Miss Edith, 166, 215
Somme, First Battle of, 177, 179, 180
Spenser, Edmund, 201
Standish, Miles, 146
Stael, Mme. de, 125
Steevens, G. W., 35
Stendhal (Henri Beyle), 17
——, *Rouge et le Noir*, 138
Stern, Miss G. B., 65
"Stevenson, George" (pseud.), 65
——, *Benjy*, 65
Stevenson, R. A. M., 35
Stevenson, R. L., 13, 17, 35, 75, 119
——, *Kidnapped*, 17
——, *Travels in the Cevennes*, 75
Strong Situation: its uses and abuse, 41–4
Sussex village names, 73
Symbolistes, 137
Swinburne, A. C., 39, 123, 147, 148, 160
Symons, Arthur, 26, 56, 200–1
——, *London Nights*, 201

T

"Technique," 10, 79–85
Tennyson, Alfred, Lord, 13, 164
Terrail, P. du, 86
Terry, Miss Ellen, 47
Thackeray, W. M., 43
Thompson, Francis, 199
Thrush, 25
To-Day, 38
Tomlinson, W. H., 136
Trade Unions, the Best of, 52

Tradition, Poems of the Great; their composition, 145-7
Trelawny, E. J., 191-2, 193
——, Recollections of . . . Shelley and Byron, 191-2
——, Records of Shelley, Byron, and the Author, 191
Tuebingen, 169, 170, 172, 217
Tupper, Martin, 20, 187
Turgenev, Ivan, 17, 22, 31, 39, 57, 88, 104, 105, 110, 114-5
——, Bielshin Prairie, 70
——, Fathers and Children, 88, 138
——, House of Gentlefolk, 99
——, Rattle of the Wheels, 70
——, Singers, 70
——, Sportsman's Sketches, 70
Twain, Mark, 113
——, Yankee at the Court of King Arthur, disliked by Henry James, 113

V

Vauxhall Gardens, 25
Vega, Lope da, 16
Velasquez, 174
Verlaine, P., 200
Vers Libre, 60; Stephen Crane and, 110; indulged in by Cubists, etc., 149, 185-215
Victoria, R. et I., 219-220
Villon, 150, 162, 172
Virgil, 13
Vittori, F., 1
Vorticists, 25, 40, 60, 62, 137-140, 149, 174

W

Wadsworth, H., 61, 64, 174
Wagner, R., 82
Wallas, Graham, 187, 194
——, Life of Place, 187, 194
Ward, Mrs. Humphry, 124
Washington, D. C., 115-6
Watson, Marriott, 35
Watts, Isaac, D.D., 188
Wauch, Professor, 5

Wearing of the Green, 189, 190
Webster, J., 100
——, Duchess of Malfi, 100
Wedmore, Sir F., 35
Wells, H. G., 26, 56, 59
Wharton, Mrs. E., 105
Wheatsheaf (C.P.R.), 173
Whibley, G., 35
Whistler, J. McN., 102
Whitman, Walt, 198
Wilde, O., 7, 9, 38, 146, 199
William III. (of England, etc.), 6
Williams, William Carlos, 104; quoted, 158, 159, 166
Winchelsea, 35, 47, 113, 114, 124
Wister, Owen, 69, 112
Winterhausen, Professor (imaginary), 218
Wood, Mrs. Henry, 86
Woolf, Mrs. Virginia, 65
Wordsworth, W., 13, 14, 191, 195; quoted, 224
——, Excursion, 224
Wounds, Self-Inflicted, 3
Writer, Typical English, his intoxication, 9, 12, 13; his triumph, 38; his dislikes, 49
Wyllarde, Miss Dolf, 87

X

X, Mr., 20-21; his determination to suppress Messrs. Pound and Flint, 135, 195

Y

Y, Mr., 20, 134; his determination to suppress Messrs. Flint and Pound, 195
Yeats, W. B., 26, 56, 187, 194
——, Innisfree, 187, 190, 194
Yellow Book, 36-39, 57, 58, 65, 66, 199

Z

Zangwill, I., 38
Zola, E., 57

THE END